"It would be hard to overstate how i̶̶̶̶̶̶̶̶̶̶̶̶̶̶̶̶̶̶̶ ment, for evangelicals to recover a ro̶̶̶̶̶̶̶̶̶̶̶̶̶̶̶̶̶̶̶ of the most important contributions C̶̶̶̶̶̶̶̶̶̶̶̶̶̶̶̶̶̶̶̶̶̶̶̶̶̶̶̶̶ ...a is healthy local churches in which spiritu̶̶̶̶̶̶̶̶̶̶̶̶̶̶̶̶ ...a sisters gather to give glory to the triune God. In *The Church*, Gregg Allison has done the church a great service in helping us recover a robust ecclesiology that will undoubtedly serve elders, deacons, ministry leaders, and congregations. I pray this book gets the wide reading it deserves."

> **J. T. English,** Lead Pastor, Storyline Fellowship, Arvada, Colorado; author, *Deep Discipleship*

"What is the church? Ask your friends, and you'll get a legion of answers. In the face of such confusion, Gregg Allison's volume *The Church* provides a clear and concise explanation—one based on decades of thoughtful study and experience. Allison considers practices that are common to Christians and on which we differ. His book is a readable, illuminating, trustworthy guide to ecclesiology that will inform your mind and kindle your soul."

> **Chris Castaldo,** Lead Pastor, New Covenant Church, Naperville, Illinois; author, *Talking with Catholics about the Gospel*

"Maintaining a proper ecclesiology is as vital now as ever. Gregg Allison's work here is rich yet concise, intelligent yet accessible. *The Church* ought to be a primary resource for both leaders in every church and students in every Christian institution."

> **Ryan Welsh,** Campus Pastor of Teaching, The Village Church, Southlake, Texas; Adjunct Instructor, Southwestern Baptist Theological Seminary; coauthor, *Raising the Dust*

"There are few men who have thought about the church as much as Gregg Allison and even fewer who have his combination of theological and practical experience. Allison's framework for examining key doctrines and practices for various expressions of the church should prove encouraging to the theologian, insightful to the pastor, and accessible to the layperson. This book is a profitable read for anyone who loves the church and cares about her future."

> **Jimmy Scroggins,** Lead Pastor, Family Church, West Palm Beach, Florida; author, *Turning Everyday Conversations into Gospel Conversations*

"I am encouraged to see a book on the doctrine of the church by Gregg Allison! It is written by a man who has not only given his life to systematic theology, including the study of the church on an academic level, but has also given his life to the church on a practical level. Allison is a churchman who loves the church. I had the blessing of seeing his love for the church up close when my wife and I were part of a small group that he and his wife led while we were attending the same church some years ago. I saw the way that he loved, discipled, and shared his life with God's people. The best people to learn from are those who are knowledgeable on the subject they are writing about and who also have practical experience. This is why you will be blessed to learn about the doctrine of the church from Gregg Allison."

T. C. Taylor, Lead Pastor, One Fellowship Church, Indianapolis, Indiana

The Church

SHORT STUDIES IN SYSTEMATIC THEOLOGY

Edited by Graham A. Cole and Oren R. Martin

The Church

An Introduction

Gregg R. Allison

CROSSWAY®

WHEATON, ILLINOIS

Parts of the introduction and the chapters in part 2 are drawn from Gregg R. Allison, "The Prospects for a 'Mere Ecclesiology,'" *Southern Baptist Journal of Theology* 23, no. 2 (2019): 61–84. Used by permission of *Southern Baptist Journal of Theology*.

Parts of chapters 2, 4, 5, and 7 are drawn from Gregg R. Allison, *Sojourners and Strangers: The Doctrine of the Church*, Foundations of Evangelical Theology (Wheaton, IL: Crossway, 2012), as marked below. Used by permission of Crossway, a publishing ministry of Good News Publishers, Wheaton, IL 60187, www.crossway.org.

Parts of chapters 4, 5, 6, and 8 are drawn from *The Baker Compact Dictionary of Theological Terms*, by Gregg R. Allison, copyright © 2016, as marked below. Used by permission of Baker Books, a division of Baker Publishing Group.

Much of the "More Baptism" section in chapter 6 is taken from Gregg R. Allison, "The Ordinances of the Church," The Gospel Coalition, Concise Theology Series, https://www.the gospelcoalition.org/essay/the-ordinances-of-the-church/. Used by permission of the Gospel Coalition.

Cover design: Jordan Singer

First printing 2021

Printed in the United States of America

Unless otherwise indicated, Scripture quotations are from the ESV® Bible (The Holy Bible, English Standard Version®), copyright © 2001 by Crossway, a publishing ministry of Good News Publishers. Used by permission. All rights reserved.

Scripture quotations marked NASB are from *The New American Standard Bible®*. Copyright © 1960, 1962, 1963, 1968, 1971, 1972, 1973, 1975, 1977, 1995 by The Lockman Foundation. Used by permission. www.Lockman.org.

Scripture quotations marked NIV are taken from the Holy Bible, New International Version®, NIV®. Copyright © 1973, 1978, 1984, 2011 by Biblica, Inc.™ Used by permission of Zondervan. All rights reserved worldwide. www.zondervan.com. The "NIV" and "New International Version" are trademarks registered in the United States Patent and Trademark Office by Biblica, Inc.™

All emphases in Scripture quotations have been added by the author.

Trade paperback ISBN: 978-1-4335-6246-4
ePub ISBN: 978-1-4335-6249-5
PDF ISBN: 978-1-4335-6247-1
Mobipocket ISBN: 978-1-4335-6248-8

Library of Congress Cataloging-in-Publication Data

Names: Allison, Gregg R., author.
Title: The church : an introduction / Gregg R. Allison.
Description: Wheaton, Illinois : Crossway, 2021. | Series: Short studies in systematic theology | Includes bibliographical references and indexes.
Identifiers: LCCN 2020016746 (print) | LCCN 2020016747 (ebook) | ISBN 9781433562464 (trade paperback) | ISBN 9781433562471 (pdf) | ISBN 9781433562488 (mobi) | ISBN 9781433562495 (epub)
Subjects: LCSH: Church.
Classification: LCC BV600.3 .A449 2021 (print) | LCC BV600.3 (ebook) | DDC 262—dc23
LC record available at https://lccn.loc.gov/2020016746
LC ebook record available at https://lccn.loc.gov/2020016747

Crossway is a publishing ministry of Good News Publishers.

V P		30	29	28	27	26	25	24	23	22	21
15	14	13	12	11	10	9	8	7	6	5	4	3	2	1

To the courageous and faithful Italian church planters
Andrea and McKenzie, Dani and Xenia, Elio and
Nicoletta, Francesco and Claudia, Franco and Priscille,
Gian Luca and Nella, Giuseppe and Rachel, Jonathan
and Annette, Leonardo and Valeria, Michel, Pippo
and Enrica, Rob and Sandy, Stefano and Jennifer.
You have enriched my life and ministry!

Contents

Series Preface

The ancient Greek thinker Heraclitus reputedly said that the thinker has to listen to the essence of things. A series of theological studies dealing with the traditional topics that make up systematic theology needs to do just that. Accordingly, in each of these studies, a theologian addresses the essence of a doctrine. This series thus aims to present short studies in theology that are attuned to both the Christian tradition and contemporary theology in order to equip the church to faithfully understand, love, teach, and apply what God has revealed in Scripture about a variety of topics. What may be lost in comprehensiveness can be gained through what John Calvin, in the dedicatory epistle of his commentary on Romans, called "lucid brevity."

Of course, a thorough study of any doctrine will be longer rather than shorter, as there are two millennia of confession, discussion, and debate with which to interact. As a result, a short study needs to be more selective but deftly so. Thankfully, the contributors to this series have the ability to be brief yet accurate. The key aim is that the simpler is not to morph into the simplistic. The test is whether the topic of a short study, when further studied in depth, requires some unlearning to take place. The simple can be amplified. The simplistic needs to be corrected. As editors, we believe that the volumes in this series pass that test.

While the specific focus varies, each volume (1) introduces the doctrine, (2) sets it in context, (3) develops it from Scripture, (4) draws the various threads together, and (5) brings it to bear on the Christian life. It is our prayer, then, that this series will assist the church to delight in her triune God by thinking his thoughts—which he has graciously revealed in his written word, which testifies to his living Word, Jesus Christ—after him in the powerful working of his Spirit.

Graham A. Cole and Oren R. Martin

Introduction

We Know the Church

We know the church.

It's the brownish-red brick building with white columns and a tall steeple just a few blocks down the street. It's the former Creamy Creations bakery whose space has been converted into a meeting place and whose storefront now bears the name New Creation. The church is the small makeshift chapel whose original galvanized iron sheets for "walls" have been replaced by white clapboard siding. It's the rented sheep pen on the farm to which the city dwellers travel two hours for its predawn meetings. The church is the grand cathedral downtown known for its architectural wonders, its beautiful stained-glass windows and mosaic artwork, and its magnificent pipe organ.

Or maybe the church is the few rural families that gather for Sunday morning worship and potluck dinner as they have done for many decades and generations. It's the thousands of anonymous suburban strangers who meet for one hour in a comfortable, state-of-the-art auditorium to hear motivational talks based loosely on biblical stories. The church is seventy-five faithful survivors of the government's antireligion purge, crammed into a three-room apartment to whisper words of hope while watching warily for spies. It's the forty people who compose the "launch team" poised to plant a new church in a largely unchurched part of the city. It's the millions of people worshiping virtually through the software platforms SecondLife or AltspaceVR.

Perhaps the church is the citizens of the nation, born into the faith because they were born in that nation. It's all the elect, those believers who are predestined by God to be his people.[1] The church is the patriarchs and old covenant believers in Yahweh—people like Abraham, Isaac, Moses, Ruth, David, Isaiah, Jeremiah, and Esther—together with the new covenant followers of Christ. It's the new covenant Christians who have been incorporated into the body of Christ through water baptism and baptism with the Holy Spirit. The church is those doubly baptized people only. It's those doubly baptized people plus their baptized children.

Or the church is especially the Roman Catholic faithful; a bit less so the Orthodox and Protestants; possibly the monotheistic Muslims and Jews; potentially Hindus, Sikhs, Buddhists, and others who follow the instructions of their religion; as well as animists, agnostics, and atheists who obey the dictates of their conscience.[2] The church is where we witness "self-sacrificing love, care about community, longings for justice, wherever people love one another, care for the sick, make peace not war, wherever there is beauty and concord, generosity and forgiveness, the cup of cold water."[3] The church is all people who have ever lived and will live, because, whether in this life or

---

1. Augustine, *On Baptism, against the Donatists*, 5.27.38, in *Nicene and Post-Nicene Fathers of the Christian Church*, 1st ser., ed. Philip Schaff (1886–1890; repr., Peabody, MA: Hendrickson, 1994), 4:477.

2. This view is the inclusivist position of the (post–Vatican II) Roman Catholic Church as explained in Vatican Council II, *Lumen Gentium*, 14–16. For further discussion, see Gregg R. Allison, *Roman Catholic Theology and Practice: An Evangelical Assessment* (Wheaton, IL: Crossway, 2014), 163–66, 175–80.

3. Clark Pinnock, *Flame of Love: A Theology of the Holy Spirit* (Downers Grove, IL: InterVarsity Press, 1996), 209–10.

after death, they have embraced or will embrace the goodness of God.[4]

Yes, we know the church!

Or, given these many notions of church, do we really? *The Church: An Introduction* will help you know the church.

Mere and More Ecclesiology

This book is part of a series, Short Studies in Systematic Theology, whose aim is for theologians to "[address] the essence of a doctrine."[5] In this case, the doctrine that I treat is *ecclesiology*.[6] This term comes from two Greek words: *ekklēsia*, "church," and *logos*, "study." Ecclesiology, then, is the study of the church. Specifically, this book, as an introduction to the doctrine of the church, is oriented to what I call *mere ecclesiology* and *more ecclesiology*.

As for *mere ecclesiology*, I don't mean several things. By *mere*, I don't mean "something that is unimportant." While not as important as the doctrines of the Trinity and Jesus Christ,[7] this doctrine is crucial in terms of our understanding and practice of the church. Nor does *mere* signify "something that is simple" in the sense of not complex, a reductionistic ecclesiology that strips down the doctrine to just a few preferred topics. And *mere* does not signal "being nothing more than" in the sense of a "lowest common denominator." Such an approach would ignore or conceal theological distinctives that tend to

---

4. This is the position of universalism, as held, for example, by David Bentley Hart, *That All Shall Be Saved: Heaven, Hell, and Universal Salvation* (New Haven, CT: Yale University Press, 2019).

5. See the "Series Preface," p. 11.

6. For a more in-depth treatment of the church, see Gregg R. Allison, *Sojourners and Strangers: The Doctrine of the Church*, Foundations of Evangelical Theology (Wheaton, IL: Crossway, 2012).

7. See treatments of these two doctrines in this Short Studies in Systematic Theology (SSST) series: Scott R. Swain, *The Trinity: An Introduction*, SSST (Wheaton, IL: Crossway, 2020); Stephen J. Wellum, *The Person of Christ: An Introduction*, SSST (Wheaton, IL: Crossway, 2021).

highlight disagreements between various ecclesiologies. That aspect falls under my label *more ecclesiology*. Therefore, a *mere ecclesiology* is not an approach that trivializes this doctrine or is reductionistic or minimizes differences of perspective on ecclesiology.

As I use it, *mere* indicates "common ground," in the sense of that which is central to the subject matter. At the same time, such core concentration does not disregard or disguise the fact that the topic is much more extensive than is its identified essence. An example of this use of *mere* is C. S. Lewis's very familiar work *Mere Christianity*.[8] Lewis writes to unbelievers, and his purpose is "to explain and defend the belief that has been *common to nearly all Christians at all times*." Appropriately, then, he intentionally avoids all disputed matters with respect to Christianity. Lewis adds this clarification: "The reader should be warned that I offer no help to anyone who is hesitating between two Christian 'denominations.' You will not learn from me whether you ought to become an Anglican, a Methodist, a Presbyterian, or a Roman Catholic." And Lewis underscores the fact that Christians "exist" not in a theoretical idea, like his proposed "mere Christianity," but in concrete churches and denominations. Indeed, for Lewis, his *Mere Christianity*

> is more like a hall out of which doors open into several rooms. If I can bring anyone into that hall I shall have done what I attempted. But it is in the rooms, not in the hall, that there are fires and chairs and meals. The hall is a place to wait in, a place from which to try the various doors, not a place to live in. For that purpose the worst of the rooms (whichever that may be) is, I think, preferable.[9]

8. C. S. Lewis, *Mere Christianity* (New York: Touchstone, 1996).
9. Lewis, *Mere Christianity*, 11–12; italics mine.

Lewis's *Mere Christianity*, then, functions as a theological construct that serves a specific purpose of highlighting essential doctrines and core practices of the Christian faith. It is the common ground shared by most Christians throughout the history of the church. It does not claim or even aim to be a description of the faith and practice of actual Christians such as Daniel Hess or Daniele Haas, or of specific existing churches such as Redeemer Presbyterian Church or Redeemer Baptist Church or Redeemer Lutheran Church or Redeemer Episcopal Church.

Lewis's employment of the term in *Mere Christianity* is a fine example of how I use *mere* in this book.[10] *Mere ecclesiology* is a theological construct that serves a specific purpose of highlighting the essential nature of the church, its core ministries, its principal leadership framework, and more. These central attributes, functions, and structures represent the common ground shared by most churches throughout history.[11] *Mere ecclesiology* does not disregard or disguise the fact that the doctrine and practice of the church is much more extensive than is its identified essence. And it does not claim or even aim to be a description of actual Presbyterian, Baptist, Lutheran, and Episcopalian ecclesiologies.

The task of addressing specific beliefs and practices of different churches and denominations is what I call *more ecclesiology*, the parallel work alongside *mere ecclesiology*. The essential

---

10. Todd A. Wilson does something similar in a different area with *Mere Sexuality: Rediscovering the Christian Vision of Sexuality* (Grand Rapids, MI: Zondervan, 2017). A recent attempt at a *mere ecclesiology*, though restricted to a magisterial Protestant perspective, is Joseph Minich and Bradford Littlejohn, eds., *People of the Promise: A Mere Protestant Ecclesiology* (Lincoln, NE: Davenant Trust, 2017).

11. For this reason, this book engages with A Reforming Catholic Confession (2017), whose notion of *mere* is similar: "What we offer is not a harmony of Protestant confessions, or an attempt to discover our lowest common doctrinal denominator, much less a charter for a new denominational entity or ecumenical organization. Rather, our statement aims at displaying an interdenominational unity in the essentials of the faith and agreement that the Word of God alone has final jurisdiction—hence 'mere' (focused on the essentials) 'Protestant' (founded on the Bible)." "Explanation: A Historical and Theological Perspective; Why We Say What We Say," art. 15, *A Reforming Catholic Confession*, accessed June 15, 2020, https://reformingcatholic confession.com/.

nature of the church, its core ministries, its principal leadership framework, and the like that represent the common ground shared by all churches are expressed in different characteristics, functions, and structures in particular churches and denominations. A few examples will suffice. All churches are directed and instructed by leaders, but particular churches are guided and taught by different types of leaders: bishops, pastors, elders, overseers, deacons, trustees, and directors. All churches have some type of governmental structure, but particular churches are organized according to different types of polities: episcopalianism is bishop led, presbyterianism is elder ruled, and congregationalism is member approving. All churches administer the rites that Jesus ordained for them, but particular churches call them by different names (ordinances or sacraments) and administer the first rite of baptism either to adults (credobaptism, for believers only) or to children (paedobaptism, for the infants of believing parents). Particular churches call the second rite by different names (the Lord's Supper, the Eucharist, Communion, or breaking of bread) and view its relationship to the presence of Christ in terms of consubstantiation, memorialism, spiritual presence, or some combination.

As an introduction to the doctrine of the church, this book addresses both *mere ecclesiology* and *more ecclesiology*. For each topic, the first section presents the common ground shared by most churches throughout history. This aspect tackles the essence, or core, of the church's identity, leadership, government, ordinances or sacraments, ministries, and future. The second section of each of these six topics describes how this essence expresses itself in the actual practices and structures of particular churches.

Before delving into *mere ecclesiology* and *more ecclesiology*, however, I need to ground our topic in both Scripture and theology.

PART 1

Foundational Issues

1

The Triune God and the Church

In this opening part, I present the foundation for ecclesiology. Because this book is an exercise in systematic theology, I begin with a consideration of the triune God and the church. As one theologian proposes,

> The revealed secret of God not only concerns the unfathomable majesty of God himself; it also concerns that human society [the church] which the triune God elects, sustains and perfects "to the praise of his glorious grace" (Eph. 1.5). From this there emerges two fundamental principles for an evangelical ecclesiology. First, there can be no doctrine of God without a doctrine of the church, for according to the Christian confession God *is* the one who manifests who he is in the economy of his saving work in which he assembles a people for himself. Second there can be no doctrine of the church which is not wholly referred to the doctrine of God, in whose being and action alone the church has its being and action.[1]

---

1. John Webster, "On Evangelical Ecclesiology," *Ecclesiology* 1, no. 1 (2004): 9.

Following this wise counsel, I turn to a discussion of the triune God and the church. I focus on three prominent biblical metaphors or images: the people of God, the body of Christ, and the temple of the Holy Spirit.

All that exists has been created by and has its being from the triune God. So it is with the church: it is the creation—or, better, the re-creation—of the God who is three-in-one. Men and women, redeemed through the gospel from "every tribe and language and people and nation" (Rev. 5:9), gather in churches and compose the people of God, the body of Christ, and the temple of the Holy Spirit throughout the world. These biblical pictures help us imagine the church as a Trinitarian re-creation.

At the heart of this affirmation is the traditional doctrine of the inseparable operations of the Trinity. That is, in every divine work—such as creation, providence, salvation, and consummation—the three persons act indivisibly. Take the work of creation as an example. The Father spoke the universe and everything in it into existence (e.g., "Let there be light," Gen. 1:3) through the Word, or the agency of his Son (John 1:1–3; Col. 1:15–16; Heb. 1:1–2), as the Holy Spirit "was hovering over the face of the waters" (Gen. 1:2) in preparation for actualizing the world.[2] Thus, though we commonly refer to the first person as Creator, the doctrine of inseparable operations signifies that creation did not come into existence apart from the work of the second and third persons as well.

So it is with the church. While we commonly associate the church with the Son—foremost in our mind is the metaphor of "the body of Christ" (1 Cor. 12:27; Eph. 4:12)—the insepa-

---

2. For further discussion of the role of the Holy Spirit in creation, see Gregg R. Allison and Andreas J. Köstenberger, *The Holy Spirit*, Theology for the People of God (Nashville: B&H Academic, 2020), 295–301.

rable operations of the Trinity mean that this re-creation does not come into existence apart from the work of the Father and of the Holy Spirit through the gospel. Indeed, the church is a Trinitarian re-creation: the people of God, the body of Christ, and the temple of the Holy Spirit.

The People of God

The people of God exist in two senses. First, human beings as created by God are his people. This image, then, relates to human beings as the only creatures who bear the divine likeness (Gen. 1:26–27). In a creation sense, all people who have ever existed, exist now, and will ever exist are rightly the people of God. As Scripture explains,

> The God who made the world and everything in it, being Lord of heaven and earth, does not live in temples made by man, nor is he served by human hands, as though he needed anything, since he himself gives to all mankind life and breath and everything. And he made from one man every nation of mankind to live on all the face of the earth, having determined allotted periods and the boundaries of their dwelling place, that they should seek God, and perhaps feel their way toward him and find him. Yet he is actually not far from each one of us, for
>
> > "In him we live and move and have our being";
>
> as even some of your own poets have said,
>
> > "For we are indeed his offspring." (Acts 17:24–28)

As the people of God in a creation sense and as divine image bearers, all human beings have dignity, worth, and significance and are to be accorded respect, honor, and love.

Second, human beings as redeemed by God are his people. This image, then, relates to Abraham and the patriarchs; the faithful remnant of Israel; Simeon and Anna, who beheld the infant Jesus; and genuine Christians in the church—to single out some examples. In a redemption sense, all people who have experienced salvation through the good news are rightly the people of God. It is in this second sense that I discuss the biblical image of the people of God.

Positively and negatively, the Old Testament focuses on the people of Israel as the people of God. One passage addresses God's establishment of Israel as his people, while a second passage rehearses the expulsion of Israel as God's people. The first narrative occurs shortly after the people were liberated from enslavement to Egypt:

> Moses went up to God. The LORD called to him out of the mountain, saying, "Thus you shall say to the house of Jacob, and tell the people of Israel: 'You yourselves have seen what I did to the Egyptians, and how I bore you on eagles' wings and brought you to myself. Now therefore, if you will indeed obey my voice and keep my covenant, you shall be my treasured possession among all peoples, for all the earth is mine; and you shall be to me a kingdom of priests and a holy nation.' These are the words that you shall speak to the people of Israel." (Ex. 19:3–6)

God established his people as called mercifully by the Lord to himself as a covenant people. By heeding the covenant, they were the Lord's treasured possession among all the rest of the people whom he created, flourishing as a priestly kingdom and a holy nation.

Sadly, the people of Israel did not heed the stipulation "if you will indeed obey my voice and keep my covenant" (Ex.

19:5). Rather, they disobeyed God's word and broke the covenant. Accordingly, God expelled them from being his covenant people. Scripture uses striking language to portray this covenant divorce: "When the LORD first spoke through Hosea, the LORD said to Hosea, 'Go, take to yourself a wife of whoredom and have children of whoredom, for the land commits great whoredom by forsaking the LORD'" (Hos. 1:2). After obeying the LORD and taking Gomer as his wife, Hosea and Gomer had a son, whose name signified the forthcoming destruction of Israel. Sometime later, "[Gomer] conceived again and bore a daughter. And the LORD said to [Hosea], 'Call her name No Mercy, for I will no more have mercy on the house of Israel, to forgive them at all'" (Hos. 1:6). As if this were not enough, Scripture continues:

> When she had weaned No Mercy, she conceived and bore a son. And the LORD said, "Call his name Not My People, for you are not my people, and I am not your God."
>
> Yet the number of the children of Israel shall be like the sand of the sea, which cannot be measured or numbered. And in the place where it was said to them, "You are not my people," it shall be said to them, "Children of the living God." (Hos. 1:8–10)

Thus, God disestablished his people because of their idolatry by forsaking the Lord. Whereas once he showed them mercy as his people, God called them "No Mercy" and "Not My People." Still, hope is sounded with the promise that God will once again take his people to himself and address them as "children of the living God."

The New Testament presents the fulfillment of this hopeful promise as taking place in Jesus Christ and those whom he saves through the gospel. He is "a living stone rejected by men but in the sight of God chosen and precious" (1 Pet. 2:4). Those whom he redeems

> like living stones are being built up as a spiritual house, to be a holy priesthood, to offer spiritual sacrifices acceptable to God through Jesus Christ. For it stands in Scripture:
>
> > "Behold, I am laying in Zion a stone,
> >   a cornerstone chosen and precious,
> > and whoever believes in him will not be put to
> >   shame." (1 Pet. 2:5–6)

Peter adds to his portrait of the people of God, harking back to the promise of Hosea:

> But you are a chosen race, a royal priesthood, a holy nation, a people for his own possession, that you may proclaim the excellencies of him who called you out of darkness into his marvelous light. Once you were not a people, but now you are God's people; once you had not received mercy, but now you have received mercy. (1 Pet. 2:9–10)

This explanation of the people of God leads to an exhortation for them:

> Beloved, I urge you as sojourners and exiles to abstain from the passions of the flesh, which wage war against your soul. Keep your conduct among the Gentiles honorable, so that when they speak against you as evildoers, they may see your good deeds and glorify God on the day of visitation. (1 Pet. 2:11–12)

Accordingly, the people of God are those who have tasted the goodness of the Lord and have come to Christ, trusting in him for redemption. Drawing on the rich Old Testament imagery of the old covenant people of God—a chosen race, a royal

priesthood, a holy nation, a people for his own possession—
Peter presents the new covenant people of God. They once were
not a people, but now they are God's people. They once had
not received mercy, but now they have received mercy. Living in
accordance with their identity, the people of God announce his
excellent characteristics and his mighty acts. Living as sojourners and strangers, they pursue holiness rather than sinfulness,
mirroring God and engaging in good works, with the result that
the enemies of God will one day glorify him.

In summary, both the Old and New Testament present the
one people of God in two aspects: as the people of Israel in old
covenant relationship with him and as the people of the church
in new covenant relationship with him. Believers constitute the
one people of God.

From this metaphor of the people of God, another characteristic of all believers must be noted: they have been elected
by God for salvation. While some people chafe at the notion
of a divine choice of certain individuals to become the people
of God, Scripture highlights and celebrates this truth. For example, the people of Israel were divinely elected, as exemplified
by God's own declaration:

> For you are a people holy to the LORD your God. The
> LORD your God has chosen you to be a people for his trea-
> sured possession, out of all the peoples who are on the face
> of the earth. It was not because you were more in number
> than any other people that the LORD set his love on you
> and chose you, for you were the fewest of all peoples, but
> it is because the LORD loves you and is keeping the oath
> that he swore to your fathers, that the LORD has brought
> you out with a mighty hand and redeemed you from the
> house of slavery, from the hand of Pharaoh king of Egypt.
> (Deut. 7:6–8)

Here divine election stands in contrast with human worthiness and merit to be the recipients of God's favor. God's gracious election is the only reason for Israel's establishment and redemption as the Lord's covenant people.

The New Testament confirms this electing action on God's part. As the gospel spreads to the Gentiles through his ministry, Paul confronts a pressing question: Has God rejected the people of Israel whom he elected? Pointing to himself as a Jew who is now saved by God, Paul forcefully denies that God has abandoned his elect. For further support, he appeals to Elijah, who despaired for the people of Israel. Even then, through divine election, the Lord preserved seven thousand faithful Israelites. From this past account, Paul draws an application for his own day: "So too at the present time there is a remnant, chosen by grace. But if it is by grace, it is no longer on the basis of works; otherwise grace would no longer be grace" (Rom. 11:5–6). God, who graciously chose the people of Israel, continues to save a remnant of Jews. The elect still obtain salvation by grace.

In accordance with God's plan, his electing work has now been extended to the Gentiles. To the church in Ephesus, composed largely of Gentiles, Paul writes about God the Father choosing the Ephesian believers in Christ before the foundation of the world (Eph. 1:4), predestining them for adoption as his sons through Christ "according to the purpose of his will" (Eph. 1:5), just as he "works all things according to the counsel of his will" (Eph. 1:11). Thus, Christ has

> made us both [Jews and Gentiles] one and has broken down in his flesh the dividing wall of hostility . . . , that he might create in himself one new man in place of the two, so making peace, and might reconcile us both to God in one body through the cross, thereby killing the hostility. (Eph. 2:14–16)

The new covenant church, composed of both Jews and Gentiles, is the elect people of God.

To summarize, from the beginning of the world, God creates human beings in his image, thereby constituting them as the people of God in the sense of creation. Additionally, God re-creates certain human beings whom he has elected eternally, thereby constituting them as the people of God in the sense of salvation. Specifically, this redeemed people of God consists of two aspects: the people of Israel in old covenant relationship with him and the people of the church in new covenant relationship with him. Believers constitute the one people of God.

The Body of Christ

A second prominent biblical metaphor of the church as a Trinitarian re-creation is the body of Christ. Specifically, "Christ is the head of the church, his body, and is himself its Savior" (Eph. 5:23). The church as Christ's body was inaugurated after the completion of the incarnate Son's saving work—his death, burial, resurrection, and ascension—as Paul explains:

> [God the Father] raised [Christ] from the dead and seated him at his right hand in the heavenly places, far above all rule and authority and power and dominion, and above every name that is named, not only in this age but also in the one to come. And he put all things under his feet and gave him as head over all things to the church, which is his body, the fullness of him who fills all in all. (Eph. 1:20–23)

Exalted as head over all created things, the Son as cosmic head was installed as head of his body, the church.

This metaphor portrays several key matters for the church. As the body, the church submits to Christ, its head. It is the church of Jesus Christ (Matt. 16:18–19) and does not belong to any individual or corporate institution. And the church depends on the loving direction and provision of its head. An application is that the church, especially its leaders, seeks constantly to discern the will of the Lord Jesus for its many ministries. It halts ministries that are no longer fruitful. It modifies ministries that need an overhaul. It starts new ministries to meet changing challenges. The church repudiates any and all agendas other than those that correspond to Christ's will for it.

Moreover, the metaphor depicts the constitution of the church: it is a diverse body with many parts united to one another. Its diversity is seen in two realms. One realm is its people. Members of the church span a spectrum as broad as the demographic in which it is located. The biblical presentation of such diversity highlights this mixture of people: Jews and Greeks, slaves and free, men and women, young and old (Acts 2:17–18; Gal. 3:26–28). Today, in any given city in which the church exists, additional elements of diversity will include different ethnicities, different socioeconomic levels, different educational backgrounds, different cultures and customs, different kinship ties, different languages, and different political persuasions.

A second realm is the diversity of spiritual gifts. Detailed discussion follows later. Suffice it to note now that the church celebrates and depends on a wide variety of giftedness. Teachers, leaders, prophets and prophetesses, givers, helpers, administrators, healers, exhorters, discerners—all are needed for the maturity and multiplication of the church. Against our sinful tendency toward jealousy and toward having a sense of either superiority or inferiority, Paul chides,

> For the body does not consist of one member but of many. If the foot should say, "Because I am not a hand, I do not belong to the body," that would not make it any less a part of the body. And if the ear should say, "Because I am

not an eye, I do not belong to the body," that would not make it any less a part of the body. If the whole body were an eye, where would be the sense of hearing? If the whole body were an ear, where would be the sense of smell? But as it is, God arranged the members in the body, each one of them, as he chose. If all were a single member, where would the body be? As it is, there are many parts, yet one body. (1 Cor. 12:14–20)

Accordingly, the church is composed of many diverse members who work together and use their diverse gifts to build up the body (Eph. 4:11–16).

The metaphor additionally pictures the types of relationships that should mark Christians in the church. As members of one another (Rom. 12:4; Eph. 4:25), they are brothers and sisters in Christ (1 Tim. 5:1–2). Only when the church functions as a family is it able to obey Jesus's new commandment of love (John 13:34–35). Only when church members are characterized by siblingship can they engage in the "one anothers" so prominent in Scripture: prayer, harmony, acceptance, patience, burden bearing, confession of sin, service, truth telling, likemindedness, humility, hospitality, unity, and more. Only when the church denounces and refuses to be characterized by hypersexualization can its male and female members stop being suspicious of one another and stop treating one another as sexual predators and seductresses.[3] Only when the church embodies the reality of being brothers and sisters in Christ can it actualize this vision: "that there may be no division in the body, but that the members may have the same care for one another. If one member suffers, all suffer together; if one member is honored, all rejoice together" (1 Cor. 12:25–26).

---

3. For further discussion, see Gregg R. Allison, *Embodied: Living as Whole People in a Fractured World* (Grand Rapids, MI: Baker, 2021), chap. 4.

Finally, the metaphor of the body of Christ is itself beautifully portrayed by the ordinance or sacrament of the Lord's Supper. When the church administers this rite, its presiding officer breaks one loaf of bread and elevates one cup of wine, thus powerfully symbolizing the unity of the body joined together in fellowship with its Lord and head: "The cup of blessing that we bless, is it not a participation in the blood of Christ? The bread that we break, is it not a participation in the body of Christ? Because there is one bread, we who are many are one body, for we all partake of the one bread" (1 Cor. 10:16–17). The body of Christ is properly a united church beautifully symbolized as its members stream forward to partake of the Communion elements and participate together in the Lord's Supper.

Unlike the first metaphor, the people of God, and like the third metaphor, the temple of the Holy Spirit (our next discussion), the metaphor of the body of Christ applies only to the community of Christians who constitute the new covenant church. That is, it does not apply to the old covenant people of Israel. As we have seen, the inauguration of the body of Christ awaited the career of the long-awaited Messiah / suffering servant: in the words of the Nicene-Constantinopolitan Creed, God the Son, "for us and for our salvation, came down from heaven, and was incarnate of the Holy Spirit and the virgin Mary, and was made man; and was crucified also for us under Pontius Pilate, and suffered and was buried; and the third day he rose again, according to the Scriptures; and ascended into heaven, and sits at the right hand of the Father." Only at his session, at the position of authority, did the God-man, Jesus Christ, as the head of all things, become head of his body, the church (Eph. 1:20–23). Consequently, the metaphor of the body of Christ applies only to the new covenant church.

Importantly, this restricted application of the metaphor does not mean that the new covenant church was not foreshadowed by the old covenant people of Israel. As they were saved by God's grace, which they embraced by faith in his promised safety scheme, so too are the members of the church graciously rescued as they appropriate the provision of Christ's atoning sacrifice for their sins. Abraham is the quintessential example, the prototype of such justification (Rom. 4). Moreover, God made his old covenant people aware of a future in which that covenant, weakened by their disobedience and with a built-in obsolescence, would give way to a second and better covenant (Jer. 31:31–34). The mediator of this new covenant would be the Messiah, the suffering servant, who would be anointed and empowered by the Holy Spirit (Isa. 11:2; 42:1; 61:1–3; Luke 4:18–19). Unlike the experience of the old covenant people of Israel, on whose leaders—judges, kings, prophets—the Spirit would come for temporary empowerment, the new covenant people would experience a fresh, unprecedented outpouring of the Spirit, whose presence would remain with them forever (Joel 2:28–32, cited in Acts 2:16–21; John 7:35–37; 14:16–17; 15:26; 16:7–15).

This foreshadowing is at the heart of James's appeal to the prophecy of Amos at the Jerusalem Council. As the church listened to testimonies of the gospel's spread among the Gentiles, James explained,

> With this the words of the prophets agree, just as it is written,
>
> > "After this I will return,
> > and I will rebuild the tent of David that has fallen;
> > I will rebuild its ruins,
> > and I will restore it,

that the remnant of mankind may seek the Lord,
　　and all the Gentiles who are called by my name,
　　says the Lord, who makes these things known
　　　　from of old."

Therefore my judgment is that we should not trouble those
of the Gentiles who turn to God. (Acts 15:14–19, citing
Amos 9:11–12)

This turning of the Gentiles to the Lord in the new covenant
was hinted at before Christ, yet it largely remained a mystery.
What had been distantly rehearsed became directly "revealed to
his holy apostles and prophets by the Spirit," the mystery "that
the Gentiles are fellow heirs, members of the same body, and
partakers of the promise in Christ Jesus through the gospel"
(Eph. 3:5–6).

This foreshadowing is also at the heart of the appeal to
the Old Testament in support of Jesus's close association with
members of the new covenant church. As the letter to the He-
brews explains of Jesus, who shares with sinful people in their
humanity and suffering,

He is not ashamed to call them brothers, saying,

"I will tell of your name to my brothers;
　　in the midst of the congregation [Gk. *ekklēsia*]
　　　I will sing your praise."

And again,

"I will put my trust in him."

And again,

"Behold, I and the children God has given me."
　　(Heb. 2:11–13)

The author's use of the word *ekklēsia*, "congregation" or "church," and his use of the familial language of "brothers" (and sisters) and "children" do not indicate that the church as the body of Christ existed prior to his coming. As we have seen, this could not be the case. Rather, it means that the psalmist (Ps. 22) and the faithful prophet Isaiah along with his disciples (Isa. 8:16–18)—both of whom are cited in this text—looked forward to the day when God would constitute his new covenant people of God through Jesus Christ, the long-awaited Messiah and the fulfillment of prophecy.

In summary, the New Testament presents the church as the body of Christ. It is the new covenant people who are being re-created through the gospel of Christ, who, as "the head of the church, his body, . . . is himself its Savior" (Eph. 5:23).

The Temple of the Holy Spirit

A third principal biblical metaphor of the church as a Trinitarian re-creation is the temple of the Holy Spirit. As Paul presses the Corinthian church, "Do you not know that you are God's temple and that God's Spirit dwells in you? If anyone destroys God's temple, God will destroy him. For God's temple is holy, and you are that temple" (1 Cor. 3:16–17).

The outpouring of the third person of the Trinity on the day of Pentecost gave birth to the church as the temple of the Holy Spirit. As such, the metaphor applies only to the new covenant people of God. Not only is the church re-created as the people of God by Christ, who on its behalf accomplished salvation, it is also re-created by the Holy Spirit, who on behalf of the church applies the saving work of Christ as announced in the gospel. In terms of individual believers, the Spirit's mighty acts include conviction of sin (John 16:7–11); regeneration (John 3:1–8; Titus 3:5–8); union with Christ (Rom. 8:9–10); justification

(1 Cor. 6:11); adoption (Rom. 8:14–15; Gal. 4:4–7); baptism with the Spirit (1 Cor. 12:13); sealing, down payment, guarantee, and first fruits (2 Cor. 1:22; 5:5; Eph. 1:13–14; 4:30); assurance of salvation (Rom. 8:16); sanctification (1 Pet. 1:1–2); and glorification and resurrection (Rom. 8:11).[4]

In terms of the corporate church, the re-creative work of the Holy Spirit includes giving birth to new churches, empowering the church for its missional engagement (Acts 1:8, exemplified by the church of Antioch sending out, in step with the Spirit's command, Barnabas and Paul on their first missionary journey; Acts 13:1–4), establishing leaders (Acts 20:28), distributing and empowering spiritual gifts to church members (1 Cor. 12:7, 11), and more. Indeed, as R. E. O. White puts it, "The church is above all else the locus of the Spirit; her origin, direction, authority, expansion, and development are directly the Spirit's concern, and her members are those upon whom the Spirit has 'fallen' or 'been poured.'"[5]

But what does it mean for the church to be the temple, the dwelling place of God? For background to this image, I turn first to the Old Testament ideas of God's presence and temple.

God's creation of the first human beings as his image bearers (Gen. 1:26–28) was accompanied by his placement of them in the garden of Eden (Gen. 2:8, 15, 22). In one sense, this place was a garden-temple, in which the Lord dwelt together with Adam and Eve in full and open relationship.[6] Tragically, this harmony was shattered by the fall into sin, to which God responded with the punishment of expulsion:

---

4. For further discussion of the Holy Spirit and salvation, see Allison and Köstenberger, *The Holy Spirit*, 367–414.

5. R. E. O. White, *The Biblical Doctrine of Initiation* (Grand Rapids, MI: Eerdmans, 1960), 189.

6. G. K. Beale, *The Temple and the Church's Mission: A Biblical Theology of the Dwelling Place of God*, New Studies in Biblical Theology 17 (Downers Grove, IL: InterVarsity Press, 2004).

> Therefore the LORD God sent him out from the garden
> of Eden to work the ground from which he was taken.
> He drove out the man, and at the east of the garden of
> Eden he placed the cherubim and a flaming sword that
> turned every way to guard the way to the tree of life. (Gen.
> 3:23–24)

Being banished from the divine presence, Adam and Eve could no longer dwell in God's garden-temple. They became outcasts in a wasteland, displaced far from God.

And so arose the crucial question, one that continues to reverberate throughout the rest of Scripture: How will God once again dwell with his people?

The Old Testament answers that question with a partial solution and a promised expectation. First, the Lord instructed Moses about the consecration of the tabernacle built according to divine design, promising, "I will *dwell* among the people of Israel and will be their God. And they shall know that I am the LORD their God, who brought them out of the land of Egypt that I might *dwell* among them. I am the LORD their God" (Ex. 29:45–46; cf. Lev. 26:11–13). The tabernacle was a temporary structure in which God dwelt with his people.

Next, the Lord instructed Solomon to build a temple. At the conclusion of the construction, the priests brought the ark of the covenant into the temple. Scripture records that "when the priests came out of the Holy Place, a cloud filled the house of the LORD, so that the priests could not stand to minister because of the cloud, for the glory of the LORD filled the house of the LORD" (1 Kings 8:10–11). At first in the tabernacle, now in the temple, God dwelt among his people.

After Israel's idolatrous rebellion against him, the Lord sent his people into exile, displaced from the land of his blessing.

Even upon their return and the building of the postexilic temple, the glorious presence of God did not return with them and dwell there. What the Lord gave instead was a prophetic hope that he would intervene decisively through his Spirit-anointed servant and restore the fortunes of his people, with whom he would once again dwell.

> I will take you from the nations and gather you from all the countries and bring you into your own land. I will sprinkle clean water on you, and you shall be clean from all your uncleannesses, and from all your idols I will cleanse you. And I will give you a new heart, and a new spirit I will put within you. And I will remove the heart of stone from your flesh and give you a heart of flesh. And I will put my Spirit within you, and cause you to walk in my statutes and be careful to obey my rules. You shall dwell in the land that I gave to your fathers, and you shall be my people, and I will be your God. (Ezek. 36:24–28)

This prophetic hope focused on the expectation of the Spirit of God himself dwelling within his people.

We turn next to the New Testament to see how the apostolic writings answer our crucial question: How will God once again dwell with his people? The answer centers on Jesus Christ and his work to overcome the sinfulness of fallen human beings. It begins with God the Son's incarnation and emplacement: "The Word became flesh and dwelt [like a tabernacle] among us" (John 1:14). As the ultimate temple, the fullness of deity in bodily form, Jesus cleansed the current temple, provoking a cross-examination:

> So the Jews said to him, "What sign do you show us for doing these things?" Jesus answered them, "Destroy this temple, and in three days I will raise it up." The Jews then

said, "It has taken forty-six years to build this temple, and will you raise it up in three days?" But he was speaking about the temple of his body. (John 2:18–21)

This interchange pointed to the ultimate reason for which the Son became incarnate and emplaced: to offer himself as an atoning sacrifice for sinful people, accomplishing the work required so that God could once again dwell among his people.

On the basis of his saving work, Jesus promised the presence of the Father and the Son in his disciples: "If anyone loves me, he will keep my word, and my Father will love him, and we will come to him and make our home with him" (John 14:23). Immediately before this promise, Jesus had assured his disciples: "And I will ask the Father, and he will give you another Helper, to be with you forever, even the Spirit of truth. . . . You know him, for he dwells with you and will be in you" (John 14:16–17). Thus, the presence of the Father and the Son in believers would be connected to the dwelling of the Holy Spirit in them. The triune God would once again dwell with his people by means of the Holy Spirit dwelling in Christ's disciples. Corresponding to this is Paul's piercing question, "Do you not know that your body is a temple of the Holy Spirit within you, whom you have from God? You are not your own" (1 Cor. 6:19).

The fulfillment of this promise applies not only on an individual level but on a corporate level as well. The church is the place of the presence of God and the answer to the crucial question we're asking: How will God once again dwell with his people? Pointing back to the Old Testament promise and expectation, Paul emphasizes,

What agreement has the temple of God with idols? For we are the temple of the living God; as God said,

> "I will make my dwelling among them and walk
>   among them,
>   and I will be their God,
>   and they shall be my people.
> Therefore go out from their midst,
>   and be separate from them, says the Lord,
> and touch no unclean thing;
>   then I will welcome you,
> and I will be a father to you,
>   and you shall be sons and daughters to me,
> says the Lord Almighty." (2 Cor. 6:16–18; citing
>   Ex. 29:45; Lev. 26:12; et al.)

Thus, the church as the actualization of the ancient promise and prophetic expectation is the temple of God.

On both an individual and a corporate level, the clear application is that Christians and the church denounce their sin, keep away from all ungodliness, confess and repent when they stumble, and walk in purity.

Sadly, such practice and pursuit always fall short of the divine standard of holiness. The fulfillment of the promise and meeting of the expectation is not yet complete in this present age. God's presence in the church is part of the reality of *already–not yet*: God does indeed dwell in his people, yet a more complete indwelling is still to come:

> Then I saw a new heaven and a new earth, for the first heaven and the first earth had passed away, and the sea was no more. And I saw the holy city, new Jerusalem, coming down out of heaven from God, prepared as a bride adorned for her husband. And I heard a loud voice from the throne saying, "Behold, the dwelling place of God is with man. He will dwell with them, and they will be his people, and

God himself will be with them as their God." (Rev. 21:1–3; citing Lev. 26:11–12)

It will not be until the new heaven and the new earth that God will completely fulfill his promise, when he dwells fully and eternally in his church, the new Jerusalem, the bride of Christ. Because the Holy Spirit is the perfecter of all the divine works, the church in the new heaven and new earth will be the perfected temple of the Spirit.

Unlike the first metaphor, the people of God, and like the second metaphor, the body of Christ, this metaphor of the temple of the Holy Spirit applies only to Christians who constitute the new covenant church. That is, it does not apply to the old covenant people of Israel. While there are important continuities between the earlier tabernacle and temples and the church, the discontinuities are significant. Of particular importance is the permanence of the divine presence in individual Christians and the church as compared with those former places. Moreover, as the New Testament's citations of the Old Testament promises and expectations demonstrate, those earlier locations for God's presence were shadows of and pointers to the substance and actualization of the triune God's indwelling among his new covenant people, the church, the temple of the Holy Spirit.

To be highlighted, then, are the two co-instituting principles of the church: Jesus Christ and the Holy Spirit. Through their two missions—the Father sending the Son, and the Father and the Son giving the Holy Spirit—the church as the body of Christ and the temple of the Holy Spirit is birthed, empowered, gifted, matured, and multiplied.[7]

---

7. For further discussion, see Allison and Köstenberger, *The Holy Spirit*, 273–77; Gregg R. Allison, *Sojourners and Strangers: The Doctrine of the Church*, Foundations of Evangelical Theology (Wheaton, IL: Crossway, 2012), 117–20.

In summary, ecclesiology properly begins with a consideration of the doctrine of God. Specifically, it is grounded in Trinitarian theology, which leads to this conclusion: There is one people of God, who from eternity past has graciously elected all those who will believe in him by faith and walk with him in obedience, worship, love, and service. This one people of God consists of two aspects: the people of Israel in old covenant relationship with him and the people of the church in new covenant relationship with him. Specifically in regard to this second aspect, the church is the body of Christ and temple of the Holy Spirit. As the body, the church submits to its head, celebrates its diversity of people and gifts, lives out its siblingship in all purity, and portrays and fosters its unity by participation in the Lord's Supper. As the temple of the Holy Spirit, the church in which he dwells is birthed, empowered, gifted, directed, sent, and sanctified by the Spirit.

2

The Church according to Scripture

Having grounded the theology of the church in the theology of God, I turn now to a brief sketch of the biblical framework for ecclesiology.

Old Testament

It is quite common to approach the Old Testament basis for the church by focusing on the Hebrew word *qahal* and the types of gatherings to which it refers. A primary use of *qahal* is in reference to an assembly of the people of Israel for religious purposes, as the following examples show:

- The Lord gives instructions to Moses concerning how to celebrate the Passover, specifying, "You shall keep it until the fourteenth day of this month, when the whole assembly [*qahal*] of the congregation of Israel shall kill their lambs at twilight" (Ex. 12:6).
- The Lord again directs Moses concerning the Day of Atonement and the specific responsibilities of the high

    priest, concluding, "No one may be in the tent of meeting from the time he enters to make atonement in the Holy Place until he comes out and has made atonement for himself and for his house and for all the assembly [*qahal*] of Israel" (Lev. 16:17).

- Before leaving Mount Sinai, the people of Israel are summoned by trumpet blast, signaling that "all the congregation [*qahal*] shall gather themselves to you [Moses] at the entrance of the tent of meeting" (Num. 10:3).

- For the reading of the law, Moses is told, "Gather [a form of *qahal*] the people to me, that I may let them hear my words, so that they may learn to fear me all the days that they live on the earth, and that they may teach their children so" (Deut. 4:10).

- A messianic psalm turns from cries of horror to a chorus of hope: "I will tell of your name to my brothers; / in the midst of the congregation [*qahal*] I will praise you" (Ps. 22:22).

- Through the prophet Joel, the Lord beckons his wayward people to return to him: "Blow the trumpet in Zion; / consecrate a fast; / call a solemn assembly; / gather the people. / Consecrate the congregation [*qahal*]; / assemble the elders; / gather the children, / even nursing infants" (Joel 2:15–16).

The assembly at Passover; the nation atoned for on the Day of Atonement; the gathering before Mount Sinai; the men, women, and children convened to hear the reading of God's word; the Messiah's people; the repentant congregation—these examples provide a general sense of *qahal* as a reference to the whole assembly of the people of God gathered for religious purposes.

At the same time, *qahal* may refer to a group of people who are together but not for religious purposes:

- The massive horde of Israelites who escaped from Egypt only to be stranded in the wilderness complain to the Lord who liberated them, "You have brought us out into this wilderness to kill this whole assembly [*qahal*] with hunger" (Ex. 16:3).
- Job suffers so desperately that he beseeches the crowd around him: "I stand up in the assembly [*qahal*] and cry for help" (Job 30:28).
- In the proverb "One who wanders from the way of good sense / will rest in the assembly [*qahal*] of the dead" (Prov. 21:16), *qahal* refers to the underworld, the domain of the deceased.

The massive horde of complaining Israelites, the crowd that Job implores, a realm or domain—these examples demonstrate that the concept (perhaps even the denotation) of *qahal* is much broader than a reference to a religious gathering.

Importantly for our discussion, the Hebrew word *qahal* is often translated by the Greek word *ekklēsia*.[1] For example, in the narrative of Solomon's blessing of the people at the dedication of the temple, the Hebrew text reads, "All the assembly [*qahal*] of Israel stood," and the Greek text reads, "All the congregation [*ekklēsia*] of Israel stood" (1 Kings 8:14). In English translations, *ekklēsia* is frequently rendered "church." The lesson commonly drawn from this study is that *ekklēsia* bears a strong similarity to *qahal* and thus should be understood to refer to a gathering of Christians to worship the Lord, hear his word, pray, and so forth. As we have already seen, however, this

---

1. On many occasions it is translated by the Greek word *synagōgē*, from which we derive the term *synagogue*.

transfer from the Hebrew *qahal* to the Greek *ekklēsia* is not as straightforward as some would make it appear.

Caution, then, is urged in moving from the Old Testament notion of gatherings of the people of Israel to the New Testament idea of the church. Indeed, as Steven Wedgeworth rightly notes,

> There is no singular Old Testament institution which fully encapsulates the church. The church brings together aspects of various Old Testament concepts, and it breaks the rules of several of those concepts along the way. As such, it is not possible to identify any one of Israel's social or political structures as being "the church."[2]

Thus, while we may desire a situation in which we can point and say "there is the church" as we survey the Old Testament, such a simplistic approach is wrongheaded.

New Testament

The New Testament's presentation of the church comes in various types of writing: narrative, Gospel, letter, and apocalypse. An example of narrative is Luke's portrayal of the church birthed on the day of Pentecost. It is preceded by three stories: the outpouring of the Holy Spirit (Acts 2:1–21), Peter's preaching of the gospel (Acts 2:22–36), and the crowd's positive response of repentance and submission to baptism (Acts 2:37–41). Luke then narrates,

> And they devoted themselves to the apostles' teaching and the fellowship, to the breaking of bread and the prayers. And awe came upon every soul, and many wonders and

2. Steven Wedgeworth, "Finding Zion: The Church in the Old Testament," in *People of the Promise: A Mere Protestant Ecclesiology*, ed. Joseph Minich and Bradford Littlejohn (Lincoln, NE: Davenant Trust, 2017), 56–57.

signs were being done through the apostles. And all who believed were together and had all things in common. And they were selling their possessions and belongings and distributing the proceeds to all, as any had need. And day by day, attending the temple together and breaking bread in their homes, they received their food with glad and generous hearts, praising God and having favor with all the people. And the Lord added to their number day by day those who were being saved. (Acts 2:42–47)

This inaugural church of Jerusalem was characterized by hearing the gospel, a response of repentance and faith, baptism, instruction, community, the Lord's Supper, prayer, sacrificial giving, hospitality, worship, and missional fruitfulness.

Such was the initial fulfillment of Jesus's promise/prophecy presented in the Gospel of Matthew. After Peter confessed that Jesus is "the Christ, the Son of the living God," Jesus replied,

Blessed are you, Simon Bar-Jonah! For flesh and blood has not revealed this to you, but my Father who is in heaven. And I tell you, you are Peter, and on this rock I will build my church, and the gates of hell shall not prevail against it. I will give you the keys of the kingdom of heaven, and whatever you bind on earth shall be bound in heaven, and whatever you loose on earth shall be loosed in heaven. (Matt. 16:16–19)

By virtue of his confession of Jesus's identity, Peter was the rock on whom Jesus promised to erect his church.[3] Through the proclamation of the gospel by Peter (and the other apostles), the initial installment of the church was the church of Jerusalem.

---

3. Gregg Allison, "What Does 'This Rock' Refer to in Matthew 16:18?," The Gospel Coalition, January 16, 2020, https://www.thegospelcoalition.org/article/what-does-this-rock-refer-to-matthew-1618/.

A few of the apostles wrote letters that addressed the doctrine and life of the churches that arose from such gospel proclamation. As we have seen, Paul highlights the work of Christ to overcome the entrenched hostility between Jews and Gentiles. Writing to the once-alienated latter group, Paul explains,

> So then you are no longer strangers and aliens, but you are fellow citizens with the saints and members of the household of God, built on the foundation of the apostles and prophets, Christ Jesus himself being the cornerstone, in whom the whole structure, being joined together, grows into a holy temple in the Lord. In him you also are being built together into a dwelling place for God by the Spirit. (Eph. 2:19–22)

Indeed, Old Testament language and imagery, once used exclusively to describe the old covenant people of Israel, is now applied to the new covenant church consisting mostly of Gentiles. As Peter explains,

> But you are a chosen race, a royal priesthood, a holy nation, a people for his own possession, that you may proclaim the excellencies of him who called you out of darkness into his marvelous light. Once you were not a people, but now you are God's people; once you had not received mercy, but now you have received mercy. (1 Pet. 2:9–10)

As the recipient of divine mercy, the church looks and strives forward to its glorious future. In an apocalyptic vision, John portrays the future church as

> the holy city, new Jerusalem, coming down out of heaven from God, prepared as a bride adorned for her husband. And I heard a loud voice from the throne saying, "Behold, the dwelling place of God is with man. He will dwell with

them, and they will be his people, and God himself will be with them as their God." (Rev. 21:2–3)

Accordingly, by means of narrative, Gospel, letter, and apocalypse, the New Testament vividly pictures the church. Given this richly textured presentation, we are not limited to merely looking at all the passages in which the Greek word *ekklēsia* appears. Neither are we dependent on making the (rather tenuous) connection between the Hebrew *qahal*, the Greek *ekklēsia*, and the English *church*. Still, in its many ways, the New Testament commonly addresses the entity that we most naturally call *church*, the gathering or assembly of Christ's followers. As I explain elsewhere,

> Specifically, these gatherings may be part of the church in a particular city that assembles regularly together in members' homes—for example, the house of Prisca and Aquila (Rom. 16:5; 1 Cor. 16:19), the house of Nympha (Col. 4:15), Philemon's house (Philem. 2), and Mary's house (Acts 12:12). These smaller gatherings were also called churches, but so were the whole church gatherings (1 Cor. 11:17, 18, 20, 33; e.g., the "whole church" that Gaius hosted, Rom. 16:23), possibly a reference to the "city" churches from which these assemblies were distributed: "the church of the Thessalonians" (1 Thess. 1:1; 2 Thess. 1:1) or "the church of God that is in Corinth" (1 Cor. 1:1–2; cf. 2 Cor. 1:1).[4]

Thus, the earliest church gatherings were largely meetings in the homes of Christians.

In addition to this aspect, another element of the church is its universality—that is, the church is the sum of all Christ followers everywhere in the world. This universal church is

---

4. Gregg R. Allison, *Sojourners and Strangers: The Doctrine of the Church*, Foundations of Evangelical Theology (Wheaton, IL: Crossway, 2012), 62.

the entity for which Christ died (Eph. 5:25). It is this church
that Christ promised to build (Matt. 16:18) and of which he is
the cornerstone (Eph. 2:20; 1 Pet. 2:6–8). It is this church that
originally existed "throughout all Judea and Galilee and Sa-
maria" (Acts 9:31) and that now exists throughout India, Iran,
and China. It is the entity that enjoys its very own category—
Paul commands that no offense should be given "to Jews or to
Greeks or to the church of God" (1 Cor. 10:32)—making it a
people who are distinct from all other peoples. In one sense,
then, there is "the church" and there is "the world."

One other New Testament passage extends the notion of
church beyond local entities and the universal reality throughout the world. Called the "heavenly church," it appears in this
vision of worship in heaven:

> But you have come to Mount Zion and to the city of the
> living God, the heavenly Jerusalem, and to innumerable
> angels in festal gathering, and to the assembly of the first-
> born who are enrolled in heaven, and to God, the judge of
> all, and to the spirits of the righteous made perfect, and to
> Jesus, the mediator of a new covenant, and to the sprinkled
> blood that speaks a better word than the blood of Abel.
> (Heb. 12:22–24)

The referent of "the assembly of the firstborn" is the church,
that is, all Christ followers who have died, become disembodied
in the intermediate state, and are currently in the presence of
God. There they join in celebratory worship with the uncount-
able angels and "the spirits of the righteous made perfect," a
reference to the entirety of old covenant believers in Yahweh.
Together with local churches and the universal church, this
"heavenly church" awaits eagerly the return of Jesus Christ and
its future reality as "the holy city, new Jerusalem, coming down

out of heaven from God, prepared as a bride adorned for her husband" (Rev. 21:2).

By combining these various presentations, we have a minimal concept of the church. It is Christ followers who (1) on a local level, worship, mature, and evangelize together as a particular church; (2) on a global level, constitute the universal church of all who embrace the gospel; (3) when deceased, become part of the heavenly church, enjoying rest from their earthly labors and worshiping the Lord face-to-face; and (4) long for Christ's return and their participation in their wedding to the Lamb.

Focusing on the first aspect, I will present the church in terms of its local expression according to the following topics: identity, leadership, government, ordinances or sacraments, ministries, and future. For each topic, the first section—*mere ecclesiology*—presents the common ground shared by most churches throughout history. This aspect addresses the essence, or core, of the church's identity, leadership, government, ordinances or sacraments, ministries, and future. The second section—*more ecclesiology*—describes how this essence expresses itself in the actual identity, leadership, government, ordinances or sacraments, ministries, and future of particular churches.

PART 2

Mere Ecclesiology and
More Ecclesiology

3

The Identity of the Church

The topic of the church's identity tackles the nature of the church in terms of its attributes, characteristics, or identity markers. I explore both *mere identity*—what all churches believe about and practice in relation to the nature of the church—and *more identity*, with specific attention given to the different notions of the attributes of the church according to the Roman Catholic Church and Protestant churches.

Mere Identity

The early church's creeds offer the following affirmations:

- Apostles' Creed: "I believe in the holy catholic church."
- Nicene-Constantinopolitan Creed: "We believe in one, holy, catholic, and apostolic church."

Importantly, both creeds confessed their ecclesiological belief in terms of the essence or attributes of the church rather than its ministries or roles. In part, this emphasis had to do with the church's aim to define itself over against heretical groups that had separated themselves from the church while still claiming to be genuine churches.[1] Of note are four essential identity markers: oneness, holiness, catholicity, and apostolicity.

Oneness

The church is characterized by unity, especially in relation to sound doctrine. As Irenaeus affirmed early on,

> The church, though dispersed throughout the whole world, even to the ends of the earth, has received from the apostles and their disciples this faith . . . [and] as if occupying one house, carefully preserves it. It also believes these points [of sound doctrine] just as if it had only one soul, and one and the same heart. It proclaims them, teaches them, and hands them down, with perfect harmony, as if it possessed only one mouth.[2]

This attribute of oneness finds substantial biblical support, from Jesus's high priestly prayer that his followers be united (John 17:11, 21–23) to Paul's insistence that the Holy Spirit grants unity to the church, especially with regard to being one body with one Spirit, hope, Lord, faith, baptism, and Father (Eph. 4:1–6; cf. 4:13). The church, then, is identified by its oneness, especially its unity in doctrine.

Holiness

Unlike the world and its character of sinfulness, the church is characterized by holiness. This purity is positional, in the sense that the holy church is set apart for, or consecrated to, God

---

1. For further discussion, see Gregg R. Allison, *Historical Theology: An Introduction to Christian Doctrine* (Grand Rapids, MI: Zondervan, 2011), 567–69.

2. Irenaeus, *Against Heresies*, 1.10.1–2, in *Ante-Nicene Fathers* (henceforth *ANF*), ed. Alexander Roberts (Peabody, MA: Hendrickson, 1994), 1:330–31. The text has been rendered clearer.

and his purposes. Regretfully, the church is not always and everywhere empirically identifiable as holy, given its continued sinfulness as part of its living a liminal existence—already but not yet pure. This matter-of-fact unholiness did not stop early church leaders from calling their members to break from their sinfulness and pursue purity, underscoring this attribute. As Justin Martyr intoned, "Let it be understood that those who are not found living as Christ taught are not Christians, even though they profess with the lips the teachings of Christ."[3] Aware of the fragmentary nature of its present holiness, the church yearns for its future unveiling as "the holy city, new Jerusalem," the radiant bride of Christ, clothed in his perfect holiness (Rev. 21:2).

Biblical support for this attribute includes references to the church as a sanctified, saintly assembly (1 Cor. 1:2; cf. 1 Pet. 2:9) and exhortations to the church to live as a holy people (1 Pet. 1:14–16). Therefore, an identity marker of the church is its holiness.

Catholicity

Rather than referring to the particular Roman *Catholic* Church, *catholicity* refers to the church's universality (Gk. *katholikos,* "universal"). The church is catholic because of (1) the presence of Christ in it and (2) the universal commission given to it by Christ. Regarding the first reason, Ignatius offered, "Where there is Christ Jesus, there is the Catholic Church."[4] As for the second reason, Christ commissioned his disciples with the following order: "Go therefore and make disciples of all nations,

---

3. Justin Martyr, *First Apology,* 16, in *ANF,* 1:168. The text has been rendered clearer.

4. Ignatius, *Letter to the Smyrneans,* 8 (shorter version), in *ANF,* 1:90. Later, Irenaeus would add, "Where the church is, there is the Spirit of God; where the Spirit of God is, there is the church." Irenaeus, *Against Heresies,* 3.24.1, in *ANF,* 1:458.

baptizing them in the name of the Father and of the Son and of the Holy Spirit" (Matt. 28:19). This Great Commission is universal in scope. As explained by Cyril of Jerusalem, the church is catholic because

> it extends over all the world . . . and Because it teaches universally and completely one and all the doctrines which ought to come to men's knowledge . . . and because it brings into subjection to godliness the whole race of mankind . . . and Because it universally treats and heals the whole class of sins . . . and possesses in itself every form of virtue which is named, both in deeds and words, and in every kind of spiritual gifts.[5]

In contrast to a peculiar splinter church (like that of Donatus or Novatian), the true church is catholic. Consequently, Ignatius issued a warning: "Whoever does not meet with the congregation [Gk. *ekklēsia*, 'church'] thereby demonstrates his arrogance and has separated [or judged] himself."[6] As already noted, this characteristic of universality is well supported biblically by Jesus's Great Commission (Matt. 28:18–20; Luke 24:44–49; Acts 1:8), with the corollary that people who seek to divide the church are to be removed from the church (e.g., Rom. 16:17–18; Titus 3:10–11). They are an impediment to its universality, which is an attribute of the church.

Apostolicity

The church is characterized by adherence to the teachings of the apostles. Such apostolicity stands in contrast with heretical

---

5. Cyril of Jerusalem, *Catechetical Lectures*, 18.23, in *Nicene and Post-Nicene Fathers of the Christian Church*, 2nd ser., ed. Philip Schaff and Henry Wace (1890–1900; repr., Peabody, MA: Hendrickson, 1994), 7:139–40.

6. Ignatius, *Letter to the Ephesians*, 5, in *ANF*, 1:51.

groups, which invent and promote false doctrine. As Tertullian explained,

> From this we draw up our rule. Since the Lord Jesus Christ sent the apostles to preach, our rule is that no others ought to be received as preachers than those whom Christ appointed. . . . Now, what they preach—in other words, what Christ revealed to them—can . . . properly be proved in no other way than by those very churches which the apostles founded in person. They declared the gospel to them directly themselves, both *viva voce* [by live voice] . . . and subsequently by their writings. If, then, these things are so, it is equally clear that all doctrine which agrees with the apostolic churches—those matrixes and original sources of the faith—must be considered truth, undoubtedly containing that which the churches received from the apostles, the apostles from Christ, and Christ from God.[7]

Churches founded by the apostles in the early Christian movement were custodians of sound doctrine; thus, they were to be heeded. In turn, these apostolic churches planted other churches—second-generation apostolic churches—and so the line continued.[8] Heretical groups did not possess such a lineage; they were not able to trace their origins to first-generation apostolic churches and, more importantly, to the apostles themselves. Accordingly, they were false churches.

Most importantly, the church is apostolic in the sense of adhering to the teachings of the apostles, as those doctrines and practices were written down in Scripture. This idea of apostolicity has firm biblical support, from the foundational role of the

---

7. Tertullian, *Prescription against Heretics*, 21, in *ANF*, 3:252. The text has been rendered clearer.
8. Tertullian, *Prescription against Heretics*, 32, in *ANF*, 3:258.

apostles (Eph. 2:20) to the authoritative instructions given by the apostles (1 Cor. 14:37; 2 Thess. 2:15; 3:4, 6, 10, 12; Titus 1:3; 2 Pet. 2:3). By heeding this apostolic teaching, the church demonstrates its characteristic of apostolicity.

In summary, the early church's creedal confession of the identity markers of the church—oneness/unity, holiness/purity, catholicity/universality, and apostolicity—represents a historical precedent of the *mere identity* of the church.

More Identity

As the church progressed through the first millennium and a half, the concept of these four attributes changed, often as a digression rather than a progression. Indeed, arising out of this early church confession is *more identity*, the uniqueness of the Roman Catholic Church and of Protestant churches.

Roman Catholicism

Within Roman Catholicism, these four attributes experienced a significant transformation.

Oneness

The *oneness* of the church became centered not only on common doctrines, some of which came to deviate significantly from Scripture and the early church's faith, but also on two other factors. The first was a common liturgy, which became oriented toward the clergy, who performed it, and away from the laity, who passively participated in it. The second factor was a common leadership structure, which became hierarchical, concentrated in the papacy, and more and more corrupt. As the only church that possesses the concrete bonds of a common faith, a common liturgy, and a common hierarchy, the Roman Catholic Church emphasized the claim that it alone is the true church of Christ.[9] Specifically, "the sole Church of Christ . . . subsists in [Lat. *subsistit in*] the Catholic Church, which is governed by the successor of Peter and by the bishops in communion with him."[10] As a corollary, it is only through the Catholic Church, as "the universal help toward salvation, . . . [that] the fullness of the means of salvation can be obtained."[11]

Of course, this Roman Catholic claim of oneness resulted in a denunciation of Protestant churches at the time of the Reformation. Over time, as relationships thawed between Catholics and Protestants, the implication of this attribute came to mean that Protestant assemblies cannot legitimately be called "churches," as there is only one true church: the Roman Catholic Church. Instead, Protestants gather in "ecclesial communities";[12] even the benefits of salvation that these communities enjoy are communicated to them through the Roman Catholic Church.

Holiness

In the face of growing worldliness in the church, *holiness* became associated with certain castes of Christians: clergy (bishops, priests), religious (monks, nuns), and saints. Through

---

9. Over against heretical and splinter churches, Cyprian proclaimed, "There is no salvation out[side] of the church." Cyprian, *Letter* 72.21, in *ANF*, 5:384. He specified, "The spouse of Christ cannot be adulterous; she is uncorrupted and pure. She knows one home; she guards with chaste modesty the sanctity of one couch [bed]. She keeps herself for God. She appoints the sons whom she has borne for the kingdom. Whoever is separated from the church and is joined to an adulteress, is separated from the promises of the church; nor can he who forsakes the church of Christ attain to the rewards of Christ. He is a stranger; he is profane; he is an enemy. He can no longer have God for his Father, who has not the church for his mother. If anyone could escape who was outside the ark of Noah, then he also may escape who shall be outside of the church." Cyprian, *Treatise*, 1.6, in *ANF*, 5:423.

10. *Catechism of the Catholic Church* (New York: Doubleday, 1995), §816, citing Vatican Council II, *Lumen Gentium*, 8.2.

11. *Catechism of the Catholic Church*, §816.

12. Joseph Cardinal Ratzinger, *Dominus Iesus*, 17 (August 6, 2000); Pope Benedict XVI, "Responses to Some Questions regarding Certain Aspects of the Doctrine of the Church" (July 10, 2007).

participation in Holy Orders, the Roman Catholic clergy are transformed by the infusion of divine grace so that their very essence is of a different quality from that of the laity. By this conveyance of a sacred power,[13] they are able to perform their sacerdotal duties in the person of Christ the head so that it is Christ "who through the Church baptizes, teaches, rules, looses, binds, offers, sacrifices."[14] With their vows of poverty, chastity, and obedience, Catholic religious distinguish themselves in holiness from the ordinary lot of the Catholic faithful.[15] In terms of saints, some of the faithful "have practiced heroic virtue and lived in fidelity to God's grace" and thus are canonized as saints.[16] Through the infusion of grace, their essence has been sanctified so that their holiness distinguishes them from the rest of the faithful, who are to look to the saints as outstanding examples of holy people and to seek their assistance through prayer.

Catholicity

The vision of *catholicity* came to be that "the whole of reality, which is already one in essence, though . . . marred by sin, should be brought into a Catholic unity," with the key to this unity being the Roman Catholic Church and none other.[17] Catholic universality is grounded in the Church's self-identification as the prolongation of the incarnation of Jesus Christ. As the whole Christ—deity, humanity, and body—subsists in the Catholic Church, and as Christ is everywhere present, then logically the Catholic Church is universal.

---

13. *Catechism of the Catholic Church*, §1538.

14. Pope Pius XII, *The Mystical Body of Christ* (June 29, 1943), 54.

15. Gregg R. Allison, *Roman Catholic Theology and Practice: An Evangelical Assessment* (Wheaton, IL: Crossway, 2014), 198–200.

16. *Catechism of the Catholic Church*, §828.

17. Leonardo De Chirico, *Evangelical Theological Perspectives on Post–Vatican II Roman Catholicism*, Religions and Discourse 19 (New York: Peter Lang, 2003), 197.

Over time, as inclusivism crept into Roman Catholic theology, the Church began to extend its identity to all peoples everywhere. To the question "Who belongs to the Catholic Church?" the answer gradually came to be expressed in terms of concentric circles. The Catholic faithful occupy the innermost circle. Extending outward, other Christians (Orthodox and Protestant) possess many of the essential identity elements of the Roman Catholic Church but in a lesser measure. Continuing outward in concentric circles are other monotheists (Jews, Muslims), adherents of non-Christian religions (Hindus, Buddhists, Sikhs), and polytheists and animists. Further removed from the center are theists who act in accordance with the dictates of their conscience. Finally, in the outermost circle are agnostics and atheists who strive to live a good life. Even they are within the range of grace and thus are possibly saved, though they know nothing of the gospel or the Catholic Church.[18]

Apostolicity

The church extended its *apostolicity* to include an authoritative Tradition and an authoritative Magisterium, as well as added the doctrine of apostolic succession. Whereas the early church and its early medieval successor held to the sufficiency of Scripture, the fourteenth century witnessed the origin and development of the concept of additional divine revelation outside the written word of God. "At this time," as I note elsewhere, "the notion of church tradition—the unwritten teaching of Christ that was communicated orally from him to his disciples, and from them to their successors, the bishops—gained ascendancy in the Roman Catholic Church."[19] The Church eventually came

---

18. Vatican Council II, *Lumen Gentium*, 16. See Allison, *Roman Catholic Theology and Practice*, 175–80.

19. Allison, *Historical Theology*, 150.

to affirm both Scripture and Tradition. Specifically, the two means "are bound closely together and communicate one with the other. For both of them, flowing out from the same divine well-spring, come together in some fashion to form one thing and move toward the same goal."[20] Accordingly, the Church "does not derive her certainty about all revealed truths from the holy Scriptures alone. Both Scripture and Tradition must be accepted and honored with equal sentiments of devotion and reverence."[21]

The determination of both the canon of Scripture and the content of Tradition, together with the proper interpretation of both modes of divine revelation, became the exclusive privilege and responsibility of the Magisterium, or teaching office of the Church: the pope and the bishops in communion with him. These consecrated men enjoy such high honor and exercise such important duty because "the apostles left bishops as their successors" and "gave them 'their own position of teaching authority.'"[22] Thus, apostolic succession ensures that the Catholic Church is rightly led, taught, and sanctified by dutifully ordained bishops.

Protestantism

Breaking under these and other developments, the church eventually split into the Roman Catholic Church and Protestant churches, with the two branches developing disparate notions of the four attributes.

Oneness

While protesting the Catholic perspective on *oneness*, Martin Luther grounded the unity of the church in a different founda-

---

20. *Catechism of the Catholic Church*, §80, citing Vatican Council II, *Dei Verbum*, 9.
21. *Catechism of the Catholic Church*, §82, citing Vatican Council II, *Dei Verbum*, 9.
22. *Catechism of the Catholic Church*, §77, citing Vatican Council II, *Dei Verbum*, 7.

tion: "And unto the true unity of the church, it is sufficient to agree concerning the doctrine of the gospel and the administration of the sacraments."[23] John Calvin concurred with what came to be called the two marks of a true church: "Wherever we see the Word of God purely preached and heard, and the sacraments administered according to Christ's institution, there, it is not to be doubted, a church of God exists."[24] In Protestant churches, oneness or unity became centered on the preaching of the gospel and the celebration of baptism and the Lord's Supper.

Holiness

Against the Catholic notion of *holiness*, Protestant churches underscored that Scripture contradicts the idea of (even some) Christians achieving complete sanctification in this lifetime. Rather, full conformity to the image of Christ is both a blessing and a hope that awaits his return and the age to come. Moreover, Protestantism looked to church discipline as a divinely given means to maintain purity in the face of unrepentant sinful people and entrenched sinful situations. Some Protestant churches even elevated church discipline to a third mark of a true church.[25]

Catholicity

The Protestant commitment to *catholicity* eventually resulted in Protestant missionary movements, fueled by Jesus's Great Commission (Matt. 28:18–20). This missional orientation remains strong for most Protestants, who reject inclusivism and bemoan the fact that such a view leads to complacency

---

23. *Augsburg Confession*, 7:1–2, in *The Creeds of Christendom*, ed. Philip Schaff (New York: Harper, 1877), 3:11–12.

24. John Calvin, *Institutes of the Christian Religion*, ed. John T. McNeill, trans. Ford Lewis Battles, Library of Christian Classics (Louisville: Westminster, 1960), 4.1.9 (2:1023).

25. See, for example, the Belgic Confession, art. 29.

and inactivity toward the billions of people who have never heard the gospel.

Apostolicity

Finally, in Protestant hands, *apostolicity* came to refer to "the church's focus on preaching, hearing, believing, and obeying the teachings of the apostles, written down in the canonical New Testament writings."[26] Protestantism rejected both Roman Catholic Tradition, authoritative teachings in addition to Scripture, and the Magisterium as the determiner and interpreter of both Scripture and Tradition. Indeed, Protestant churches emphasized the sufficiency, necessity, clarity, and sole authority of Scripture (*sola Scriptura*).

Toward a Protestant Mere Identity

This chapter began with a presentation of the church's *mere identity*: it is characterized by oneness, holiness, catholicity, and apostolicity. Despite this early church consensus, later developments in the church's understanding of these four characteristics resulted in a division into the Roman Catholic Church and Protestant churches. While both traditions voice their confession of the church as one, holy, catholic, and apostolic, each branch means something significantly different from the other.

Two contemporary examples of a Protestant *mere identity* include A Reforming Catholic Confession and the New City Catechism. I treat each in turn.

A Reforming Catholic Confession. On the eve of the five-hundredth anniversary of the Protestant Reformation, "a number of leaders from across the Protestant spectrum [came] together to honor the original vision of the Reformers by demonstrating that, de-

---

26. Allison, *Roman Catholic Theology and Practice*, 183–84.

spite our genuine differences, there is a significant and substantial doctrinal consensus that unites us as 'mere Protestants.'"[27] The outcome of that international deliberation was *A Reforming Catholic Confession* (henceforth abbreviated ARCC).[28] Two of the twelve doctrinal articles address ecclesiology.

I focus here on its article "The Church" (I address the other article, which addresses the ordinances, in chap. 6):

> We believe that the one, holy, catholic, and apostolic church is God's new society, the first fruit of the new creation, the whole company of the redeemed through the ages, of which Christ is Lord and head. The truth that Jesus is the Christ, the Son of the living God, is the church's firm foundation (Matt. 16:16–18; 1 Cor. 3:11). The local church is both embassy and parable of the kingdom of heaven, an earthly place where his will is done and he is now present, existing visibly everywhere two or three gather in his name to proclaim and spread the gospel in word and works of love, and by obeying the Lord's command to baptize disciples (Matt. 28:19) and celebrate the Lord's Supper (Luke 22:19).[29]

This *mere identity* captures several key components. ARCC uses the traditional language of the Nicene-Constantinopolitan Creed, understood according to a Protestant theological interpretation.[30] Moreover, its definition of the church is such that Protestants from either a continuity position or a discontinuity position may affirm it. In the first case, seeing more continuity

---

27. "About," *A Reforming Catholic Confession*, accessed June 15, 2020, https://reformingcatholicconfession.com/about/.

28. For the purpose of full disclosure, I was part of the team that drafted ARCC.

29. "The Confession," *A Reforming Catholic Confession*, accessed June 18, 2020, https://reformingcatholicconfession.com.

30. That this is the proper framework for interpreting the four identity markers of the church is seen by the fact that ARCC rests on the formal principle of Protestantism: *sola Scriptura*. Thus, for example, while apostolicity refers to Scripture, it cannot refer to Scripture with the Apocrypha, Tradition, the Magisterium, apostolic succession, and so forth.

between the old covenant and the new covenant, and between the old covenant people of God and the new covenant people of God, leads to the view that the church began with Abraham (or Adam). Thus, it includes "the whole company of the redeemed through the ages." In the second case, seeing more discontinuity between the covenants and God's people leads to the view that the church began at Pentecost and includes Christians only. Only Christians, baptized by Christ with the Holy Spirit (Luke 3:15–17; John 1:33; 1 Cor. 12:13), are incorporated into Christ's body with him as "Lord and head" of the church (cf. Eph. 1:19–22).

Additionally, ARCC addresses both the universal church (of which Christ is the foundation, Matt. 16:16–18; 1 Cor. 3:11) and local churches (in which two or three are gathered in his name, Matt. 18:20). Furthermore, with a strong emphasis on evangelization, ARCC condenses the function of the church to declaration and demonstration. Finally, ARCC explains that the fruit of such missional and merciful endeavors is found in people being united with a church in which, in accordance with Scripture, they are baptized and celebrate the Lord's Supper.

The **New City Catechism.** A second contemporary example of a Protestant approach to *mere identity* is the New City Catechism.[31] As Tim Keller introduces it,

> Today many churches and Christian organizations publish "statements of faith" that outline their beliefs. But in the past it was expected that documents of this nature would be so biblically rich and carefully crafted that they would be memorized and used for Christian growth and training.

---

31. This project was a joint venture between the Gospel Coalition and Redeemer Presbyterian Church, of which Tim Keller was the founding pastor. In addition to the website (http://newcitycatechism.com), see the publication *The New City Catechism: 52 Questions and Answers for Our Hearts and Minds* (Wheaton, IL: Crossway, 2017).

They were written in the form of questions and answers, and were called *catechisms* (from the Greek *katechein*, which means "to teach orally or to instruct by word of mouth").[32]

While it arose out of a need for a contemporary, broadly Reformed catechism, "the New City Catechism is based on and adapted from Calvin's Geneva Catechism, the Westminster Shorter and Larger catechisms, and especially the Heidelberg Catechism."[33]

The New City Catechism has one question devoted to the identity of the church:

> Question 48: What is the church?
>
> God chooses and preserves for himself a community elected for eternal life and united by faith, who love, follow, learn from, and worship God together. God sends out this community to proclaim the gospel and prefigure Christ's kingdom by the quality of their life together and their love for one another.[34]

The catechism focuses on three key elements of the church's *mere identity*. The church is a community of people who have been elected and saved by God. As discussed earlier, both the Old and New Testaments rehearse this eternal, divine choice of the people of God. The Old Testament describes the old covenant people of Israel as the elect, and the New Testament presents the new covenant people of the church as the elect. In every case, the people chosen by gracious favor do indeed find

---

32. Tim Keller, "Introduction," *New City Catechism*, accessed June 15, 2020, http://newcitycatechism.com/introduction-timothy-keller/.

33. Keller, "Introduction," *New City Catechism*, http://newcitycatechism.com/introduction-timothy-keller/.

34. "Question 48: What Is the Church," *New City Catechism*, accessed June 18, 2020, http://newcitycatechism.com/new-city-catechism/#48.

salvation. This is true not only of individual believers but also, as they are joined together, of the corporate community—Israel, the church.

While a gathered outpost of the kingdom of God, the church is also a scattered society of divinely sent ambassadors. They announce the good news of Christ as they live for and love one another as the gospel community. In this way, the church is multiplied throughout the world.

In conclusion, I have treated the topic of the church's identity in terms of both *mere identity*—what all churches believe about and practice in relation to the nature of the church—and *more identity*, with specific attention given to the different notions of the attributes of the church according to the Roman Catholic Church and Protestant churches.

4

The Leadership of
the Church

All churches are directed and instructed by leaders. But particular churches are guided and taught by different types of leaders. This chapter addresses the leadership of the church in terms of both *mere leadership*—what all churches believe about and practice in relation to it—and *more leadership*, with specific attention given to the offices of apostleship; bishopric, eldership, pastorate, or presbytery; and diaconate.

Mere Leadership

All churches are directed and instructed by leaders. If this were not the case, the chaos portrayed in the book of Judges would characterize churches: "Everyone did what was right in his own eyes" (Judg. 17:6).

The New Testament addresses *mere leadership* with several instructions. Congregational members are exhorted to consider and copy their leaders: "Remember your leaders, those who spoke to you the word of God. Consider the outcome of their way of life, and imitate their faith" (Heb. 13:7). Furthermore, members are directed toward a respectful submission: "Obey your leaders and submit to them, for they are keeping watch over your souls, as those who will have to give an account. Let them do this with joy and not with groaning, for that would be of no advantage to you" (Heb. 13:17). Paul echoes these teachings: "We ask you, brothers, to respect those who labor among you and are over you in the Lord and admonish you, and to esteem them very highly in love because of their work" (1 Thess. 5:12–13). In summary, congregational members are to respectfully obey their leaders, highly honor them because of their guidance and instruction, and imitate their faithfulness. Leaders in turn are to instruct members from the word of God, live exemplary lives, and shepherd the flock for whom they are accountable before the Lord.

Hearing about any type of obedience to leaders can cause concern, even fear, as church members place themselves in a vulnerable position and thus open themselves up to misdirection and abuse. But leaders in the church are not to be this way, as Jesus instructed his disciples: "The kings of the Gentiles exercise lordship over them, and those in authority over them are called benefactors. But not so with you. Rather, let the greatest among you become as the youngest, and the leader as one who serves" (Luke 22:25–26). *Mere leadership*, of the type that Jesus wills and models, is actually *mere servanthood*. Thus, while possessing the (delegated) authority that is required for them to exercise their tasks, leaders are to use their authority for building up the church according to the will of God and never mistreating or exploiting those under their care.

More Leadership

Particular churches are guided and taught by different types of leaders. Generally following New Testament instructions, most churches acknowledge several offices of church leadership: apostleship; bishopric, eldership, pastorate, or presbytery; and diaconate. Offices that, though not named in Scripture, are nonetheless practical and common are those of trustee and director.

Apostleship

The office of apostleship was by divine design a temporary position of authority in the early church.[1] As I explain elsewhere,

> Apostles are the disciples chosen by Jesus to be the foundation of his church. Foremost among these leaders were the original apostles—"the Twelve"—whom Jesus called to follow him. They were Spirit-empowered eyewitnesses of his life, death, and resurrection. Additionally, *apostle* (Gk. *apostolos*, "messenger") is used to refer to a few other leaders—Paul, Barnabas, and James.[2]

The qualifications for being an apostle were two: called to be with Jesus from the outset of his ministry (Mark 3:13–15) and an eyewitness of (at least) one of his postresurrection appearances (Acts 1:21–22).[3] During their ministry with Jesus, the apostles engaged in preaching the kingdom of God, healing

---

1. For further discussion about apostles, see Gregg R. Allison, *Sojourners and Strangers: The Doctrine of the Church*, Foundations of Evangelical Theology (Wheaton, IL: Crossway, 2012), 205–11.

2. Gregg R. Allison, *The Baker Compact Dictionary of Theological Terms* (Grand Rapids, MI: Baker, 2016), s.v. "apostle."

3. The first qualification raises a question about the apostle Paul, who was not called to be one of the original apostles at the beginning of Jesus's ministry. Paul himself emphasized that while his apostleship was unusual, the Lord had indeed called him to that office (Rom. 1:1; 1 Cor. 1:1; 2 Cor. 1:1; Gal. 1:1; Eph. 1:1; Col. 1:1; 1 Tim. 1:1, 12; 2 Tim. 1:1). As for the second qualification, Paul admitted that whereas all Jesus's other postresurrection appearances had occurred within forty days of the resurrection, the

the sick, and casting out demons (Luke 9:1–2). After Jesus's ascension and the outpouring of the Holy Spirit, the apostles preached the gospel (e.g., Acts 2:14–41; 3:11–26), planted the first churches (e.g., Acts 13–14), appointed leaders for them (e.g., Acts 14:23), provided them with apostolic instructions (e.g., Acts 15; 1 Cor. 7:17–24; 14:29–35), and, in the case of some, wrote Scripture (i.e., Matthew, John, Paul, James, and Peter). Their apostolic ministries established the foundation of the emerging early church (Eph. 2:20). Given the particularities of the apostles' qualifications and the nature of their work, once the last of them died, the office of apostleship ceased to exist.

The two (remaining) permanent offices are generally distinguished in terms of leadership and service. In terms of the former, the office of leadership is variously referred to as the bishopric, eldership, pastorate, or presbytery. In terms of the latter, the office of service is called the diaconate. The two offices are discussed in turn.

Bishopric, Eldership, Pastorate, or Presbytery[4]

For simplicity's sake, we begin by defining the term *elder* as

> one who ministers in the office of oversight, or eldership. The qualifications for elders are listed in 1 Timothy 3:1–7 and Titus 1:5–9. Elders are entrusted with four responsibilities: teaching, or communicating sound doctrine; leading, or providing overall direction; praying, especially for the sick; and shepherding, or guiding, nourishing, and protecting the church.[5]

Lord's appearance to Paul—which was his last appearance—was outside this chronological framework, being postascension (1 Cor. 15:8).

4. For further discussion about elders/pastors, see Allison, *Sojourners and Strangers*, 211–40.

5. Allison, *Baker Compact Dictionary*, s.v. "elder/eldership."

Terminology

Interchangeable New Testament terms for "elder" (Gk. *presbyteros*) include "bishop" (Gk. *episkopos*; also translated "overseer"), "presbyter" (Gk. *presbyteros*), and "pastor" (Gk. *poimēn*). Three examples demonstrate the interchangeability of "elder" and "bishop"/"overseer." When Paul convenes the leaders of the church of Ephesus (Acts 20:17–35), he calls the "elders" (Gk. *presbyteroi*, Acts 20:17) to meet him and then addresses them as "bishops"/"overseers" (Gk. *episkopoi*, Acts 20:28). Additionally, in his presentation of the office of leadership to Timothy, Paul sets forth the qualifications for "bishops"/"overseers" (Gk. *episkopoi*, 1 Tim. 3:1, 2) and when discussing their roles of ruling and teaching calls them "elders" (Gk. *presbyteroi*, 1 Tim. 5:17). Similarly, in his instructions about the office of leadership to Titus, Paul mentions the task of appointing "elders" (Gk. *presbyteroi*, Titus 1:5) and follows with the qualifications of an "overseer"/"bishop" (Gk. *episkopos*, Titus 1:7). It should be noted that some churches don't translate the Greek word *presbyteros* but simply transliterate it as "presbyter." In this case, "presbyter" is another word that is interchangeable with "elder." So "elder" = "bishop" = "overseer" = "presbyter."

What of the word "pastor" (Gk. *poimēn*), which is the most common term to refer to one who holds the office of leadership in the church? The case for the interchangeability of the above words with "pastor" is made by appeal to Peter's instructions (1 Pet. 5:1–4): the "elders" (Gk. *presbyteroi*, 1 Pet. 5:1) are to "shepherd the flock of God" (1 Pet. 5:2). "Shepherd" (Gk. *poimainō*) is the verb associated with the noun *poimēn*, or "pastor." Very literally, Peter exhorts the "elders" to "pastor" the church, thus establishing the interchangeability of the words "elder" and "pastor." So "pastor" = "elder" = "bishop" = "overseer" = "presbyter."

Qualifications

As noted above, Paul details the qualifications for these leaders in 1 Timothy 3:1–7 (as well as Titus 1:5–9):

> The saying is trustworthy: If anyone aspires to the office of overseer, he desires a noble task. Therefore an overseer must be above reproach, the husband of one wife, sober-minded, self-controlled, respectable, hospitable, able to teach, not a drunkard, not violent but gentle, not quarrelsome, not a lover of money. He must manage his own household well, with all dignity keeping his children submissive, for if someone does not know how to manage his own household, how will he care for God's church? He must not be a recent convert, or he may become puffed up with conceit and fall into the condemnation of the devil. Moreover, he must be well thought of by outsiders, so that he may not fall into disgrace, into a snare of the devil.

Following how my own church addresses these qualifications, I note five areas of requirements: call, character, competencies, chemistry, and commission.

Call. Overseers are to be called by God, and such a call is sensed by an aspiration or desire to be a leader (1 Tim. 3:1). As an overseer in my church, I have important conversations with potential overseers to determine whether they sense such a divine call on their life. A negative response does not mean that such a desire will not arise in the future, but it suspends further discussion for the time being. A positive response does not mean that those who detect that call will automatically become overseers. But it does prompt me to have conversations with my fellow overseers about moving these seemingly God-called leaders into a rigorous training program for future overseers.

Character. Elders must have a certain character. Paul generalizes this qualification by saying that they "must be above reproach" (1 Tim. 3:2). Simply put, if a charge is brought against an elder, the charge must fail. When it comes to his family life, personal traits, avoidance of negative activities, and the like, an elder is blameless. No accusation that is voiced against him will stick. Importantly, this is not a requirement of sinlessness. Indeed, elders will be leading examples of confession and repentance for their congregations.

Paul then details the specifics of this all-encompassing qualification in the list that follows. An elder must be "the husband of one wife" (1 Tim. 3:3). This requirement does *not* mean several things. First, it is not a prohibition against polygamy, though that practice is certainly forbidden by the overall voice of Scripture. Polygamy was not a major concern in Paul's day, so it is unlikely that he included it in his list.

Second, it is not a requirement that an elder be married. Elsewhere, Paul emphasizes the many advantages of celibacy. If single people are "anxious about the things of the Lord, how to please the Lord," and can render "undivided devotion to the Lord," then they seem to be good candidates for being elders. Paul does not prohibit the unmarried from being elders (1 Cor. 7:32, 35).

Third, some understand "the husband of one wife" to prohibit the divorced from becoming elders. While not dismissing the importance of considering divorce when evaluating potential leaders, this is not Paul's point here. The way the qualification is stated, it could be taken to refer to a situation of divorce only quite awkwardly. Furthermore, Paul himself permits divorce in the case of an unbelieving spouse moving to dissolve the marriage (1 Cor. 7:12–16). And Jesus allows divorce in the case of marital unfaithfulness (Matt. 19:7–9).[6] Thus, divorce in such cases does not automatically disqualify potential elders. The reason for, timing of (e.g., before becoming a Christian), and attitude concerning (e.g., repentance for a sinful choice that was made decades in the past) the divorce should be considered. As for remarriage after (even a biblically warranted) divorce, churches hold various views. But in any case, "the husband of one wife" does not address that scenario; rather, it must be decided on other grounds.

What *does* Paul mean by his qualification of "the husband of one wife"? It refers to marital faithfulness: if married, elders must be devoted covenantally to their spouses and must shun all inappropriate relationships with other people.

Character requirements for elders also include the positive elements of gravitas, stability, self-discipline, and respectability. Forbidden matters are drunkenness and addiction to alcohol (and, by extension, all mind-altering drugs like marijuana), violence (gentleness must reign in place of viciousness and aggressiveness), quarrelsomeness (bickering, contentiousness, and theological sword fighting), and greediness. This last negative element explains why elders are worthy of double honor, both respect and remuneration: they are not materialistic lovers of money who are in their leadership office for shameful gain (1 Pet. 5:2).

Competencies. In terms of competencies, pastors must be proficient in three areas: hospitality, teaching, and leadership. Pastors are to be "hospitable" (1 Tim. 3:2), not in terms of a personality trait like being outgoing or extroverted but in

---

6. Wayne Grudem proposes a third reason for divorce: self-protection from abuse. For the outline of his paper presented at the Evangelical Theological Society on November 21, 2019, see Wayne Grudem, "Grounds for Divorce: Why I Now Believe There Are More than Two," accessed June 19, 2020, http://www.waynegrudem.com/grounds-for-divorce-why-i-now-believe-there-are-more-than-two/.

terms of being a friend to strangers (Heb. 13:2). Pastors self-lessly open up their hearts and homes to others. Pastors must also be "able to teach" (1 Tim. 3:2), that is, be capable of communicating biblical truth and sound doctrine. Elsewhere, Paul expands on this competency: "He must hold firm to the trustworthy word as taught, so that he may be able to give instruction in sound doctrine and also to rebuke those who contradict it" (Titus 1:9). Thus, pastors must cherish biblical truth and sound doctrine for themselves, be capable of communicating it to others, and be able to refute people who interpret Scripture wrongly or hold to false doctrine.

Additionally, pastors must be competent in leadership (1 Tim. 3:4–5). A test case for determining such ability comes from observing their home life: "He must manage his own household well, with all dignity keeping his children submissive" (1 Tim. 3:4). If pastors are able to manage at the microcosmic level of their family, it is a good indication (though not a guarantee) that they will be competent to lead at the macrocosmic level of the church. As noted before, this requirement does not mean that pastors must be married. If they are married, their home management is a good test case for assessing their leadership competencies. If they are not married, there are other ways of testing for this ability. Examples include a teacher's classroom management skills and a business owner's ability to direct a company and treat employees well.

Elsewhere, Paul adds that the pastor's "children are believers and not open to the charge of debauchery or insubordination" (Titus 1:6). In the honor-shame culture of Paul's day, the expectation was that a man who would become a Christ follower would lead his wife, if he was married, and children, if he had any, to become Christians. As leader of his home, he would guide the others in his home to embrace his faith. After Paul's instructions to Titus in light of this cultural reality, a potential leader whose children are not believers, as demonstrated by their wayward lifestyle and defiance of his leadership, would not be competent to be a pastor. On the reverse side, pastors whose children follow Christ model what it means to possess the requisite competency to lead their church.

Two other qualifications for church leadership are maturity and reputation. As for maturity, presbyters must not be recent converts (1 Tim. 3:6). Instead, they should demonstrate a significant degree of maturity in faithfulness and obedience to the Lord. While this general requirement stands, there are exceptions. Indeed, as Paul instructs Titus about appointing presbyters in newly planted churches, the apostle does not prohibit his envoy from establishing recently converted leaders in that office. In this case, Paul's counsel reflects his practice during his first missionary journey: after Barnabas and he planted churches in Antioch, Iconium, Lystra, and Derbe, they returned to those cities and "appointed elders for them in every church" (Acts 14:23). These churches were, at the most, months old. More probably, they had been launched only weeks earlier. Still, they were in need of leadership, and Barnabas and Paul established presbyters from the most mature of the new believers. Outside these pioneering situations, however, Paul's requirement that presbyters not be recent converts stands.

In terms of reputation, presbyters "must be well thought of by outsiders" (1 Tim. 3:7). When people in the neighborhood of the church think about its leaders, it is with admiration for their good reputation. Though these outsiders may vehemently oppose the Christian faith, the presbyters who hold to it and live it have the respect of those around them.

Maturity and reputation are essential for two reasons associated with the devil. Leaders who are new converts "may become puffed up with conceit and fall into the condemnation of the devil" (1 Tim. 3:6). Bearing the many responsibilities of church leadership and being fruitful in ministry, presbyters have the tendency to become arrogant. Puffed up with pride like the devil, they become susceptible to a terrible fall like that of Satan. Furthermore, presbyters must have a good reputation so that they "may not fall into disgrace, into a snare of the devil" (1 Tim. 3:7). Hypocritical leaders court shame and dishonor. They become ensnared by Satan, who uses that entrapment scheme to discredit the gospel.

Chemistry. Though the term *chemistry* does not appear in these lists of qualifications for the office of leadership, the requirement of unity among bishops is essential. Scripture places a high emphasis on unity, peace, and harmony among God's people. Jesus prays for oneness among his disciples as a reflection of the oneness of the Father and Son (John 17:20–26). Paul exhorts the church to work hard "to maintain the unity of the Spirit in the bond of peace" (Eph. 4:3) and to "complete my joy by being of the same mind, having the same love, being in full accord and of one mind" (Phil. 2:2). If the church is to obey this command and to fulfill this vision, its bishops must lead the movement toward and develop unity. Sadly, two opposing scenarios are everywhere present: (1) when its bishops are united, the church is characterized by peace and oneness; (2) when its bishops are divided, the church is characterized by discord and factionalism. Accordingly, a qualification for the office of bishop is chemistry among its leaders.

Commission. A final requirement for this office is a commission. Leaders must be affirmed by the church and publicly recognized as its officers. This commissioning is, in many cases, a solemn rite involving the laying on of hands by the other leaders. Such was the practice with Timothy: "The council of elders laid their hands on [him]" (1 Tim. 4:14). Because of the weightiness of this office, Paul warns elders, "Do not be hasty in the laying on of hands" (1 Tim. 5:22). Vetted carefully according to their call, character, competencies, and chemistry, those who serve as overseers, elders, pastors, presbyters, or bishops are brought before the church and commissioned as its leaders.

Responsibilities

As noted earlier, "elders are entrusted with four responsibilities: teaching, or communicating sound doctrine; leading, or providing overall direction; praying, especially for the sick; and shepherding, or guiding, nourishing, and protecting the church."[7] I discuss each of these four duties in turn.

Teaching. The first two responsibilities have been addressed in part under the discussion of the qualifications for eldership. Pastors must be able to teach, which includes several elements. They must treasure the word of God and the doctrine and practice that flow from it for themselves. They must convey these truths to others. And they must rebut incorrect Bible teaching and heretical doctrine. They are called, appropriately, *pastor-teachers*, or "shepherds and teachers" (Eph. 4:11). Within a church's leadership team, some of the elders will devote their time and energies especially to "preaching and teaching" (1 Tim. 5:17). Practically speaking, pastors fulfill their responsibility to teach in various ways:

> preaching during the Sunday service(s); teaching Bible studies and Sunday school classes; determining the biblical and theological content of the studies, classes, and various small group meetings (e.g., cell groups, home Bible studies, community

---

7. Allison, *Baker Compact Dictionary*, s.v. "elder/eldership."

groups); and resolving theological disputes. Furthermore, elders may shoulder this responsibility by engaging in Word-centered small-group discipleship and personal mentoring; communicating the doctrinal statement and church covenant in instructional meetings for potential new members; studying Scripture regularly as an elder team; and modeling commitment to the Word and submission to its instructions.[8]

Leading. Overseers must be able to lead the church, and they bear the responsibility to do so at the highest levels of authority. While some dedicate themselves more to preaching and teaching, all overseers work together in leading the church (1 Tim. 5:17). Their spheres of oversight, with the requisite authority to execute their duties, are teaching, leading, praying, and shepherding. Still, their authority as overseers is a delegated one: as with the whole church, its leaders are always under the supreme authority of the head of the church, Jesus Christ. Thus, they also seek to do the will of the Lord for his church. Specifically, overseers engage in

> managing the pastoral and administrative staff teams; developing the annual budget; deciding and enacting the church's philosophy of ministry; directing the process for hiring new staff; setting policies for the church; conducting congregational or church business meetings; approving new ministries; developing potential new elders; and the like.[9]

Praying. While all Christians are to pray, elders bear a particular responsibility to pray, especially for the sick:

> Is anyone among you suffering? Let him pray. Is anyone cheerful? Let him sing praise. Is anyone among you sick?

---

8. Allison, *Sojourners and Strangers*, 219.
9. Allison, *Sojourners and Strangers*, 220.

Let him call for the elders of the church, and let them pray
over him, anointing him with oil in the name of the Lord.
And the prayer of faith will save the one who is sick, and
the Lord will raise him up. And if he has committed sins,
he will be forgiven. (James 5:13–15)

When summoned by a sick church member, the elders anoint
her with oil as a sign of consecration, marking her out for the
Lord's special attention. They pray over her (accompanied often
by the laying on of hands), not only trusting that God *can heal*
her but also pleading that he *will heal* her. Praying "in the name
of the Lord" both acknowledges that the power for healing
comes from him alone and expresses the elders' submission
to God's sovereign will. With this joyful surrender as the atmosphere in which they pray, they beseech the Lord to grant
healing and expect him to do so, in accordance with his clear
promise: "The prayer of faith will save [i.e., heal] the one who
is sick." Though not all sickness is due to personal sin, there
may be cases in which it is. Thus, the elders ask the sick person
if she believes that her illness is linked to any known sin in her
life. If she responds positively, they urge her to confess her sin(s)
and then assure her of the Lord's forgiveness. As they pray,
there are three possible answers to their prayer: (1) God may
not heal the sick person, (2) he may heal her through surgical
intervention or medical treatment, or (3) God may miraculously
heal the sick person.

Shepherding. Shepherding is another pastoral duty incumbent
on these leaders: "Shepherd the flock of God that is among
you, exercising oversight, not under compulsion, but willingly,
as God would have you; not for shameful gain, but eagerly;
not domineering over those in your charge, but being examples
to the flock" (1 Pet. 5:2–3). As shepherds, they nourish their

flock with the word of God, which is the teaching responsibility already discussed. They exercise oversight, which dovetails with the leadership duty already presented. In overseeing the church, elders willingly participate according to God's will and without being coerced. They shepherd eagerly and freely, without concern for material gain. They lead in accordance with Jesus's instructions and example:

> You know that the rulers of the Gentiles lord it over them, and their great ones exercise authority over them. It shall not be so among you. But whoever would be great among you must be your servant, and whoever would be first among you must be your slave, even as the Son of Man came not to be served but to serve, and to give his life as a ransom for many. (Matt. 20:25–28)

And pastors protect their flock from dangerous yet subtle wolves and their heretical teachings (Act 20:28–31). This aspect is carried out by the faithful preaching and teaching of the word of God and through the exercise of church discipline.

In summary, the office of bishop, elder, pastor, or presbyter is held by leaders who meet the qualifications for this office and who teach, lead, pray, and shepherd.

Diaconate

The second permanent office of the church is one of service and is called the diaconate.[10] Elsewhere I explain,

> Deacons are those who serve in the office of service. From the Greek (*diakonia*, "service"; *diakonos*, "servant"), these terms are used generically to refer to anyone who engages in service and used technically for a person who is a publicly

---

10. For further discussion about deacons, see Allison, *Sojourners and Strangers*, 240–47.

recognized officer serving in a church. . . . The qualifications for men and women to serve are listed in 1 Timothy 3:8–13. Deacon responsibilities do not include leading and teaching but consist of serving in ministries.[11]

These two offices are found together in the opening lines of the letter to the Philippians, which is addressed "to all the saints in Christ Jesus who are at Philippi, with the overseers and deacons" (Phil. 1:1). Some churches distinguish the men who serve in this office from the women who serve in it by calling the former *deacons* and the latter *deaconesses*. Many churches simply use *deacons* to refer to both men servants and women servants.

Acts 6:1–7

Historically, the church has looked to Acts 6:1–7 as the biblical narrative of the inauguration of the diaconate. Dissension arose between Aramaic-speaking Jews in Palestine and Greek-speaking Jews from the outside. The issue was the distribution of food: the widows of the latter group were being overlooked in the daily rations. To free up the apostles to continue their ministry of preaching and prayer and to relieve them of taking care of this burden, the Jerusalem church chose seven men for the service of providing food to widows. These became the first deacons.

The application drawn from this passage is that pastors/elders are responsible for the spiritual ministries of the church—teaching, leading, praying, and shepherding—while deacons are responsible for physical or temporal church matters. Examples include the physical upkeep of the church building and the collection, deposit, and accounting of money.

---

11. Allison, *Baker Compact Dictionary*, s.v. "deacon/deaconess/diaconate."

Caution is urged at this point. Acts 6 actually presents both these elements—spiritual and temporal—as *ministry* or *service*. The apostles give themselves to the "ministry" (Gk. *diakonia*) of teaching the word and praying. The seven men are tasked with the service of the "daily distribution" (Gk. *diakonia*) of food. We cannot determine the nature of the ministry or service by one word alone. Indeed, *diakonia* is used to refer to both physical and spiritual work. In fact, the following narratives in Acts (chaps. 7–8) trace the careers of two of the seven deacons selected to serve in food distribution. Stephen performed signs and wonders while preaching the gospel, dying as the first Christian martyr (Acts 6:8–7:60). Philip exorcised demons, healed the sick, and preached the gospel, evangelizing many Samaritans (Acts 8:4–13) as well as the Ethiopian eunuch (Acts 8:26–40). Such *ministries* are quite different from what many churches consider to be the *services* of their deacons.

Qualifications

After his instructions about elders/overseers (1 Tim. 3:1–7), Paul addresses deacons and, as I argue below, deaconesses (1 Tim. 3:8–13):

> Deacons likewise must be dignified, not double-tongued, not addicted to much wine, not greedy for dishonest gain. They must hold the mystery of the faith with a clear conscience. And let them also be tested first; then let them serve as deacons if they prove themselves blameless. Their wives likewise [or "Women likewise," ESV mg.] must be dignified, not slanderers, but sober-minded, faithful in all things. Let deacons each be the husband of one wife, managing their children and their own households well. For those who serve well as deacons gain a good standing

for themselves and also great confidence in the faith that is in Christ Jesus.

Elsewhere I provide a breakdown of what this passage is addressing:

> Structurally, Paul begins his description of diaconal qualifications with some general characteristics of all servants (vv. 8–10), turns briefly to a specific discussion of women—either wives of deacons or deaconesses—and their qualifications (v. 11), turns to the household requirements for male deacons (v. 12), and concludes with a commendation for all servants of Jesus Christ (v. 13).[12]

Like elders/pastors, deacons must be servants with a certain character: honorable, not deceitful, not dependent on alcohol (or other drugs), and not materialistic. As for their competencies, unlike presbyters, deacons are not required to be "able to teach" (1 Tim. 3:2); as we've already seen, teaching is a responsibility of presbyters. This point should not be misunderstood to mean that deacons cannot teach. For example, a deacon of men's ministries may be a regular teacher at the Saturday morning sports outreach. In terms of their leadership competency, like presbyters, deacons are responsible for "managing their children and their own households well" (1 Tim. 3:12). This demonstrates their administrative skills. Unlike presbyters, however, who have the duty to take care of God's church (1 Tim. 3:5) and to exercise leadership at the highest level of authority, deacons use their managerial abilities for serving well. As we will see, deacons are to be leading servants.

Before they are enlisted to serve in the office of diaconate, deacons must "be tested first" (1 Tim. 3:10). "This assessment

---

12. Allison, *Sojourners and Strangers*, 243.

of deacons," Ryan Welsh and I note, "is directed at both their meeting of the character qualifications and their personal abilities. Dangerously, churches often focus on the latter evaluation giving little heed to those serving in the diaconate."[13] Indeed, deacons are allowed to serve "if they prove themselves blameless" (1 Tim. 3:10). They must first pass an evaluation of both their character and their competency. As they engage in their work, they are aware of the reward that awaits them: "Those who serve well as deacons gain a good standing for themselves and also great confidence in the faith that is in Christ Jesus" (1 Tim. 3:13). The presbyters and church members who are served well should have high regard for deacons, who in turn gain abundant assurance before their model servant, Jesus.

Churches differ on whether women can serve as deacons. To anticipate a fuller discussion later, some churches understand 1 Timothy 3:11 as giving the qualifications of the wives of deacons, while other churches interpret it as listing the qualifications of deaconesses. I return to this debate under the topic "More Ministries" (in chap. 7).

Responsibilities

At no point does Scripture set forth a list of diaconal responsibilities. Certainly, the basic idea of the office is service. At the same time, all Christians are called to serve. So how does the service of deacons and deaconesses differ from the common service that all church members are to engage in?

As discussed above, the duties of pastors are teaching, leading, praying, and shepherding. If these are pastoral responsibilities, then, as Ryan Welsh and I note,

---

13. Gregg Allison and Ryan Welsh, *Raising the Dust: "How-to" Equip Deacons to Serve the Church* (Louisville: Sojourn Network, 2019), 10–11.

deacons are responsible for leading the other, non-elder-level ministries of the church: ministries of mercy, women's ministries, men's ministries, hospitality, community groups, kids' ministries, missions, bereavement ministries, and many more. These ministries may—but not necessarily—be led by elders as well. Therefore, deacons and deaconesses are leading servants and possess and exercise the requisite authority for carrying out their responsibilities.[14]

Thus, while all members serve in the various ministries of the church, deacons and deaconesses are leading servants of those ministries.

Other Leadership Structures

Offices not named in Scripture but nonetheless practical and common include those of trustees and directors. In the case of church trustees, responsibilities may include budgetary matters and facilities. Trustees may oversee the development of the church budget, manage the collection and deposit of money (e.g., the Sunday service offerings), pay salaries and bills, ensure that the church's finances are properly audited, and maintain the church's buildings and properties. Directors may come in several varieties. If they constitute a board of directors (treating the church as a nonprofit institution), members may be involved in legal matters, in the development of church policies (e.g., conflict of interest, employee handbook, intellectual property rights), and in holding the church's buildings and other assets. Directors on a church's staff may also oversee certain ministries. In some cases, churches that restrict the office of elder/pastor to only qualified men may call women staff members "directors" of, for example, women's ministries and children's ministries.

---

14. Allison and Welsh, *Raising the Dust*, 17.

In conclusion, I have treated the topic of the church's leadership in terms of both *mere leadership*—what all churches believe about and practice in relation to it—and *more leadership*, with specific attention given to the three offices of apostleship; bishopric, eldership, pastorate, or presbytery; and diaconate.

5

The Government
of the Church

All churches have some type of governmental structure, also called polity. But particular churches are organized according to different types of polities. This chapter addresses the governance of the church in terms of both *mere government*—what all churches believe about and practice in relation to it—and *more government*, with specific attention given to the traditional polities of episcopalianism, presbyterianism, and congregationalism.

Mere Government

All churches have some type of governmental structure. Though it goes without saying, I will say it anyway: first and foremost, Jesus is the Lord of the church. He is the good shepherd, and it is his will that is sought, prayed for, and enacted by the church. The biblical case for his supreme role is straightforward.

Metaphorically, the church is presented as a building in general and a temple in particular. Speaking to Gentile Christians, Paul explains that

> you are no longer strangers and aliens, but you are fellow citizens with the saints and members of the household of God, built on the foundation of the apostles and prophets, Christ Jesus himself being the cornerstone, in whom the whole structure, being joined together, grows into a holy temple in the Lord. In him you also are being built together into a dwelling place for God by the Spirit. (Eph. 2:19–22)

There are several key components of the church's structure. Christ is the cornerstone, the principal piece that provides direction and shape to the rest of the building. The apostles and prophets are the foundation, the substructure on which the superstructure is constructed. Christians are the individual stones that, when joined together by the Holy Spirit, compose the superstructure, the building or temple of God. From this metaphor, the government of the church is implied: it is the church of Jesus Christ, and its initial human founders are the apostles and prophets.

Elsewhere in Scripture, as we have seen, Jesus himself promises, "I will build my church" (Matt. 16:18); it belongs to him. Moreover, as the ascended and exalted Lord, Jesus, the cosmic head over all things, has been given to the church as its head (Eph. 1:19–22). The headship and lordship of Christ mean that he is the one with divine authority to command, instruct, and guide the church.

We see the sovereign Lord directing his church from the very outset. Several examples will suffice. Prior to his ascension, Jesus gives his eleven disciples the Great Commission, saying,

> All authority in heaven and on earth has been given to me. Go therefore and make disciples of all nations, baptizing them in the name of the Father and of the Son and of the

Holy Spirit, teaching them to observe all that I have commanded you. And behold, I am with you always, to the end
of the age. (Matt. 28:18–20)

The resurrected Jesus is the authoritative Lord who commands
his disciples to launch what will become a worldwide church
through the millennia.

This commission is part of the mission entrusted to God the
Son by God the Father. Three days after his crucifixion, having
demonstrated to his disciples that he is resurrected, Jesus says,

> "Peace be with you. As the Father has sent me, even so I
> am sending you." And when he had said this, he breathed
> on them and said to them, "Receive the Holy Spirit. If
> you forgive the sins of any, they are forgiven them; if
> you withhold forgiveness from any, it is withheld." (John
> 20:21–23)

Jesus is at the center of this Trinitarian mission. The Father
commissioned the Son to become incarnate, live a perfect life,
be crucified, and rise again to accomplish salvation. In turn, the
Son commissions the church with the same mission but with
this difference: the church does not accomplish salvation but
announces that salvation and how to appropriate it. To fulfill
this mission, the Son signals an event that is soon to come: he
breathes, symbolizing the Spirit's outpouring on the day of Pentecost. It will be through the Spirit's presence and power that
the church, which will arise on that day, will carry the message
of salvation through Christ to the entire world. In conjunction
with the Father and the Holy Spirit, the Son incarnate both
commissions his church and is himself at the core of his church's
gospel.

We are right to speak of the church as Christ centered. It is
the church of Jesus Christ.

The church of Jerusalem, which arose initially out of Jesus's commission, was ruled by the apostles. We see them, for example, focusing on the ministry of the word and prayer as they lead the church (Acts 6:1–7). To continue this leadership role, they stay behind in Jerusalem at the outbreak of persecution (Acts 8:1). The Christians who are scattered evangelize the Samaritans, whose incorporation into the church, made up of only Jews at that point, is verified and blessed by Peter and John, two of the apostles (Acts 8:14–17). Peter leads Gentiles to Christ (Acts 10:1–11:18).

With the establishment of Paul as an apostle, the mission to the Gentiles begins in haste. Traveling with Barnabas, the two apostles plant churches and appoint elders in every church (Acts 14:23). By this time, even the Jerusalem church has elders who, together with the apostles, play an important role at the Jerusalem Council (Acts 15:4, 6, 22–23; 16:4). This new leadership structure—eldership or pastorate—becomes the pattern for all churches: while the pastors don't replace the apostles, they exercise the role as leaders responsible for teaching, leading, praying, and shepherding local churches. The appointment of elders in churches was made by both apostles and apostolic representatives (Titus 1:5). Deacons join bishops (Phil. 1:1) as leading servants.

I have yet to mention an important group of people who in some way contributed to its government: church members. Since I will return to this topic shortly, one example suffices: joining the apostles and elders at the Jerusalem Council were the members of the Jerusalem church (Acts 15:4). Their role seems to have been that of affirming the decision of the apostles and elders (Acts 15:22).

Accordingly, the early church's government was structured with Christ as head of the church; the apostles as (temporary) authoritative rulers commissioned by Christ; bishops, elders, pastors, overseers, or presbyters as leaders of local churches; deacons as servants in local churches; and members as affirming collaborators. With this sketch of Scripture's *mere government*, everyone is in general agreement.

More Government

Particular churches are organized according to different types of polity, with three traditional forms: episcopalianism, presbyterianism, and congregationalism.[1]

Episcopalianism

Episcopalianism is government by an *episkopos* (Gk.), or "bishop," in whom ultimate authority resides. In the Anglican and Methodist denominations, for example, a three-tiered polity with varying degrees of authority exists:

bishop	ultimate authority
presbyters/priests	second-order authority
deacons	supportive service

Bishops possess ultimate authority, as seen in their consecration of other bishops and their ordination of presbyters/priests and deacons. They exercise their authoritative role over numerous local churches within their jurisdiction, which is often a particular geographical area. Presbyters/priests are ordained by bishops. They minister in a local church by leading worship, preaching, praying, and administering the sacraments. Deacons are ordained by bishops and serve both them and the presbyters/priests.

---

1. For further discussion of these three polities, see Gregg R. Allison, *Sojourners and Strangers: The Doctrine of the Church*, Foundations of Evangelical Theology (Wheaton, IL: Crossway, 2012), 254–95.

This three-tiered ministry appeals to both Scripture and early church polity structure. As for the former, particular attention is paid to Paul's relationship to his representatives, Timothy and Titus, and their relationship to those whom they appointed as elders. A prototype of a bishop was James, who exercised the key leadership role in the Jerusalem church and at the Jerusalem Council. These biblical "seeds" developed rather quickly into the monarchical bishopric, that is, bishop-ruled church.

Indeed, church history confirms that early in the second century, through the influence of Ignatius, monepiscopacy (literally, "one bishop") developed as a form of church government. In a pragmatic move to ward off heresy and to maintain unity in the church, Ignatius urged that each local church should be ruled by one bishop in conjunction with the presbyters and deacons. As I explain elsewhere,

> In one sense, both the bishop and the elders exercised authority over the church. However, Ignatius also elevated the office of bishop over that of elder; the position of deacon was under both of these offices. He set up a parallel: "Be eager to do everything in godly harmony, the bishop presiding in the place of God and the presbyters in the place of the council of the apostles and the deacons." Thus, a three-tiered hierarchy was erected, with the bishop exercising ultimate authority.[2]

This monepiscopal polity was later reinforced by Cyprian in the third century. Again, he focused on the office of bishop for maintaining the unity of the church: "The bishop is in the church and the church is in the bishop. If anyone is not with the

---

2. Allison, *Sojourners and Strangers*, 257. The citation is from Ignatius, *Letter to the Magnesians*, 6, in *The Apostolic Fathers: Greek Texts and English Translations*, ed. Michael W. Holmes (Grand Rapids, MI: Baker, 1999), 153; cf. *ANF*, 1:61.

bishop, he is not in the church. The church, which is catholic [universal] and one, is . . . connected and bound together by the cement of bishops who cohere with one another."[3]

Accordingly, episcopalianism is a well-established church polity.

Presbyterianism

A second traditional variety of church government is *presbyterianism*. This version is government by *presbyteroi* (Gk.), or "elders"/"presbyters," as representatives of the church. Denominational examples include the Presbyterian Church in America and the Christian Reformed Church. Unlike the three-tiered structure of episcopalianism, presbyterianism is two-tiered, with elders/presbyters and deacons. A key reason for this twofold polity is, as we've seen, the New Testament's use of "bishop," "elder," "presbyter," "overseer," and "pastor" as interchangeable terms. Thus, following the New Testament, presbyterianism has a two-tiered government structure:

elders/presbyters	representative authority
deacons	supportive service

Presbyterian polity makes a distinction between two types of elders/presbyters: teaching elders and ruling elders. Support for this distinction is found in 1 Timothy 5:17, in which Paul distinguishes between "elders who rule well" (ruling elders) and "those who labor in preaching and teaching" (teaching elders). Teaching elders are seminary graduates, ordained by a presbytery, and responsible in a local church for the ministry of the word and the administration of the sacraments. Ruling elders are non-seminary-educated and nonordained officers who are

---

3. Cyprian, *Letter* 68.8, in *ANF*, 5:374–75.

responsible for government and discipline. Teaching elders and ruling elders lead the church.

It is at the local church level that one teaching elder (there are often more than one) and a plurality of ruling elders exercise their roles in ministry. This official leadership body is called a *session* (Presbyterian) or *consistory* (Reformed). Furthermore, as I explain elsewhere,

> All of the teaching elders and one of the ruling elders from each of the churches in a geographical area (e.g., the city of Philadelphia) form a *presbytery* (Presbyterian); alternatively, one teaching elder and one ruling elder from each church in the geographical area compose a *classis* (Reformed). The members of the presbyteries or classes in a region (e.g., the state of New Jersey) form a *synod*. Finally, teaching elders and ruling elders selected by the presbyteries from their members form on the national level a *general assembly* (Presbyterian).[4]

Each level of government, consisting of some combination of teaching and ruling elders from lower structures, has its own responsibilities. How these higher and lower bodies relate to each other in terms of authority differs from denomination to denomination.

As for biblical support for these different levels of government, the narrative of the Jerusalem Council (Acts 15) plays an important role. It portrays one presbytery (the churches of Antioch, Acts 15:2–3) requesting a conference with other presbyteries (the churches of Syria and Cilicia, Acts 15:23, 41). These bodies, who are represented by their appointed delegates (e.g., Paul and Barnabas, Acts 15:2; perhaps "Judas called Barsabbas, and Silas," Acts 15:22, cf. 15:27, 32), come together for

---

4. Allison, *Sojourners and Strangers*, 264–65.

a synod with the presbytery of Jerusalem (Acts 15:2, 4, 6) and make an authoritative decision for all the churches.

Accordingly, presbyterianism is a well-established church polity.

Congregationalism

A third traditional polity is *congregationalism*, which is government by the local congregation, in whose members ultimate authority resides under Christ. Examples of congregational polity include Baptist churches, Bible churches, and free churches (e.g., the Evangelical Free Church of America). This governmental structure differs significantly from the former two versions. As I note elsewhere,

> Each church is an autonomous entity, with no person (a bishop, as in episcopalianism) or structure (a presbytery or synod, as in presbyterianism), except for Christ, above it. Congregationalism is based on two principles: (1) autonomy, that is, each church is independent and self-governing, being responsible for its own leadership, finances, buildings, and ministries; and (2) democracy, that is, authority in each church resides in its members, who together participate in congregational decisions through some process of affirmation or denial.[5]

While the emphasis is on autonomy and independence, some congregational denominations and churches also champion collaboration and interdependence.[6]

---

5. Gregg R. Allison, *The Baker Compact Dictionary of Theological Terms* (Grand Rapids, MI: Baker, 2016), s.v. "congregationalism."

6. An example is the Southern Baptist Church, which as a denomination encourages cooperation between its member churches. Such mutual aid is detailed in its Baptist Faith and Message (2000), article 14, "Cooperation": "Christ's people should, as occasion requires, organize such associations and conventions as may best secure cooperation for the great objects of the Kingdom of God. Such organizations have no authority over one another or over the churches. They are voluntary and advisory bodies designed to elicit,

Biblical support for congregationalism includes the following: Joining the apostles and elders at the Jerusalem Council were the members of the Jerusalem church (Acts 15:4). Their role seems to have been that of affirming the decision of the apostles and elders (Acts 15:22). Additionally, according to Jesus's instructions, the church as a whole plays an important role in the final stages of church discipline (Matt. 18:15–20). An example of this function is the incestuous man (1 Cor. 5:1–5) whom Paul urged the Corinthian church to excommunicate. Apparently, the decisive verdict was carried out by "the majority" of the church members (2 Cor. 2:6). Moreover, when the expelled man repented of his heinous sin, Paul exhorted the church to "turn to forgive and comfort him" (2 Cor. 2:7).

Congregational members also played an important role in the selection of the seven men often considered to be the first deacons serving in the Jerusalem church. Although the apostles supervised this situation, they charged the "full number of the disciples" with the responsibility to "pick out from among" themselves seven qualified men whom the apostles would "appoint to this duty" (Acts 6:2–3). Similarly, members of the Antioch church sent out Paul and Barnabas for their missionary journey (Acts 13:1–3; 14:24–28). The congregation exercised an important role in the church.

This important role continued in the early centuries of the church's existence. As we have seen, monepiscopacy had its early proponents; so too did congregationalism. For example, Clement of Rome, writing to the church of Corinth, rebuked

---

combine, and direct the energies of our people in the most effective manner. Members of New Testament churches should cooperate with one another in carrying forward the missionary, educational, and benevolent ministries for the extension of Christ's Kingdom. Christian unity in the New Testament sense is spiritual harmony and voluntary cooperation for common ends by various groups of Christ's people. Cooperation is desirable between the various Christian denominations, when the end to be attained is itself justified, and when such cooperation involves no violation of conscience or compromise of loyalty to Christ and His Word as revealed in the New Testament."

the congregation for unjustly removing some elders who had been appointed to their office "with the consent of the whole church."[7] The *Didache* calls for Christians to "appoint for yourselves bishops and deacons worthy of the Lord."[8]

Accordingly, congregationalism is a well-established church polity.

Varieties of Traditional Structures and New Versions of Polity

Over time, the three traditional government structures have developed different varieties. Episcopalianism runs the gamut from the Roman Catholic Church, with its pope, cardinals, bishops, priests, and deacons, to certain Pentecostal denominations, whose bishops exercise very limited authority over the churches under their jurisdiction. As we've already seen, the presbyterian polity expresses itself differently between Presbyterian churches and Reformed churches, not only in terms of nomenclature but also in terms of the number of authoritative structures. Congregationalism also exhibits a wide variety. Some churches are led by a solo pastor with a board of deacons, which in many cases functions as a team of other pastors. Elder-*ruled* congregationalism is almost an oxymoron, as such churches give almost no say to their members. Thus, it is more common to find elder-*led* congregational churches. In such cases, the pastors/elders possess the requisite authority to exercise their roles of teaching, leading, praying, and shepherding. Likewise, deacons and deaconesses hold the authority that is necessary for them to minister as leading servants. And church members have the authority to carry out their responsibilities, which often include affirming the budget, new elders/pastors,

7. Clement of Rome, *The Letter of the Romans to the Corinthians*, 44, in Holmes, *Apostolic Fathers*, 78–79; cf. ANF, 1:16.

8. *Didache*, 15, in Holmes, *Apostolic Fathers*, 266–67; cf. ANF, 7:381.

changes to the constitution and bylaws, major property and facility purchases, new members, and the excommunication (and reaffirmation, when appropriate) of wayward members.

Finally, beginning in the twentieth century, new versions of church polity have come on the scene. An example is the church leadership structure that resembles contemporary business models. The lead pastor is like a CEO, board members function like directors of a corporation, and the members are treated like shareholders who vote with their attendance and their money. Another example is the church whose members are wary and tired of traditional authoritarian structures and thus claim to have no leaders and no polity. This laissez-faire model may privilege a charismatic atmosphere in which any participant, sensing the leading of the Holy Spirit, may speak words of direction to the church to follow.

Not to be lost in this, at times, bewildering confusion of church governmental structures is the fact that in churches of all stripes people can find oneness, holiness, catholicity, apostolicity, gospel preaching, celebration of baptism and the Lord's Supper, and genuine Christians exhibiting faith, hope, and love. Polity is not the essence of the church, but it can contribute to the well-being of the church.

In conclusion, I have treated the topic of the church's governance in terms of both *mere government*—what all churches believe about and practice in relation to it—and *more government*, with specific attention given to the traditional polities of episcopalianism, presbyterianism, and congregationalism.

6

The Ordinances or Sacraments of the Church

All churches administer the rites that Jesus ordained for them. But particular churches call these rites either ordinances or sacraments, administer the first of them to different categories of people, and celebrate the second of them according to different names and understandings. This chapter addresses the ordinances or sacraments of the church in terms of both *mere ordinances or sacraments*—what all churches believe about and practice in relation to *mere baptism* and *mere Communion*—and *more ordinances or sacraments*. In terms of *more baptism*, specific attention is given to the divergences between paedobaptism and credobaptism. As for *more Communion*, particular consideration is directed to the differences between transubstantiation (the Roman Catholic view), consubstantiation (or sacramental union), memorialism, and spiritual presence.

Mere Ordinances or Sacraments

All churches administer the rites that Jesus ordained for them. For help with the discussion of *mere ordinances or sacraments*,

I turn again to the two contemporary confessional examples of A Reforming Catholic Confession (ARCC) and the New City Catechism. I treat each in turn.

A Reforming Catholic Confession

In addition to its section "The Church" (discussed in chap. 3), ARCC includes a rather lengthy section titled "Baptism and Lord's Supper":

> We believe that these two ordinances, baptism and the Lord's Supper, which some among us call "sacraments," are bound to the Word by the Spirit as visible words proclaiming the promise of the gospel, and thus become places where recipients encounter the Word again. Baptism and the Lord's Supper communicate life in Christ to the faithful, confirming them in their assurance that Christ, the gift of God for the people of God, is indeed "for us and our salvation" and nurturing them in their faith. Baptism and the Lord's Supper are physical focal points for key Reformation insights: the gifts of God (*sola gratia*) and the faith that grasps their promise (*sola fide*). They are tangible expressions of the gospel insofar as they vividly depict our dying, rising, and incorporation into Jesus' body ("one bread . . . one body"—1 Cor. 10:16–17), truly presenting Christ and the reconciliation he achieved on the cross. Baptism and the Lord's Supper strengthen the faithful by visibly recalling, proclaiming, and sealing the gracious promise of forgiveness of sins and communion with God and one another through the peace-making blood of Christ (1 Cor. 11:26; Col. 1:20).[1]

ARCC echoes the traditional language of Protestantism's "two marks of a true church": preaching the gospel—the pro-

---

1. "The Confession," *A Reforming Catholic Confession*, accessed June 23, 2020, https://reformingcatholicconfession.com.

claimed or verbal word—and administering the two ordinances or sacraments—the enacted or visual word.[2] Both baptism and the Lord's Supper are the "visible elements that are sufficient and necessary for the existence of a true church."[3] That is, where these ordinances are celebrated along with the proclamation of the gospel, a true church exists.

Moreover, these sacraments receive their validity through association with the word of God and the Spirit of God. This point stands against the notion of *ex opere operato*, which is the Roman Catholic belief that baptism and the Lord's Supper (as well as the five other Catholic sacraments) are valid and effective simply by being administered. Historically, Protestant theology has rejected *ex opere operato* and has insisted instead on the validity and effectiveness of the ordinances as being due to their connection to the gospel and faith in it as the message of salvation.

Additionally, the fruits of both these ordinances are the communication of spiritual life, the confirmation of salvation, and the furtherance of sanctification. That is, both baptism and the Lord's Supper nourish the church for its pilgrimage in this world. To those being baptized, the sacrament provides assurance of the forgiveness of their sins. To those participating in Communion, the ordinance confirms that they belong to the crucified Christ in whose meal they share. Moreover, in both cases, the church's progress in purity and its journey toward complete sanctification is enhanced.

Furthermore, these two rites function to portray tangibly the divine bestowal and promise of grace, together with the human response of faith. The Protestant *solas* of grace alone and faith

---

2. See "Oneness" (p. 56), in chap. 3, for relevant citations from the Augsburg Confession and John Calvin's *Institutes*.

3. Gregg R. Allison, *The Baker Compact Dictionary of Theological Terms* (Grand Rapids, MI: Baker, 2016), s.v. "marks of the church."

alone are highlighted in these celebrations. Baptism vividly pictures identification with the death, burial, and resurrection of Christ (Rom. 6:3–6). The Lord's Supper strikingly depicts communion with Christ's body and blood, as well as the unity of church members in one body (1 Cor. 10:16–17).

Finally, with a nod to the various Protestant understandings of the meaning of these rites,[4] ARCC affirms three points. With John Calvin, ARCC highlights spiritual presence: to those who participate in the Lord's Supper, Christ and his salvific benefits are truly presented (1 Cor. 10:16). With Huldrych Zwingli, ARCC emphasizes commemoration: participants recall to mind Christ and his work on their behalf (Luke 22:19; Rom. 6:3; 1 Cor. 11:25–26). With Martin Luther, ARCC underscores promise: through faith in Christ's testament, participants in this sacrament are confirmed as being forgiven of their sins and being in fellowship with God and the community of faith.

With these broad areas of sacramental commonality, Protestants realize happily that the typical charge that their churches are hopelessly divided when it comes to the ordinances is incorrect, or at least needs serious tempering. All Protestant churches celebrate two sacraments. Together with the preaching of the gospel, baptism and the Lord's Supper are the two marks of a true church. Valid and effective through their association with the word of God and embraced by faith, these ordinances provide great blessing and benefit to the church.

The New City Catechism

Another example of a *mere ordinances or sacraments* proposal, representing a broad swath of evangelicalism, is the New City Catechism. One of its questions treats these church rites in general:

---

4. Stylized as representative of the three main Reformers: Calvin, Zwingli, and Luther.

Question 43: What are the sacraments or ordinances?

The sacraments or ordinances given by God and instituted by Christ, namely baptism and the Lord's Supper, are visible signs and seals that we are bound together as a community of faith by his death and resurrection. By our use of them the Holy Spirit more fully declares and seals the promises of the gospel to us.

The catechism underscores the broad consensus of evangelical churches with respect to these two rites. Baptism and the Lord's Supper are divinely given and instituted, not mere human inventions or conventions. They vividly portray and guarantee the unity of the church, the truth of the gospel, and the assurance of salvation.

The New City Catechism addresses the first rite:

Question 44: What is baptism?

Baptism is the washing with water in the name of the Father, the Son, and the Holy Spirit; it signifies and seals our adoption into Christ, our cleansing from sin, and our commitment to belong to the Lord and to his church.

The catechism emphasizes that "only the blood of Christ and the renewal of the Holy Spirit can cleanse us from sin" (question 45). Still, this cleansing is vividly portrayed when someone is baptized with water in the name of the triune God. Moreover, baptism strikingly depicts and guarantees our incorporation into the family of God while expressing our allegiance to Christ and his church.

The New City Catechism addresses the second rite:

Question 46: What is the Lord's Supper?

Christ commanded all Christians to eat bread and to drink from the cup in thankful remembrance of him and his

> death. The Lord's Supper is a celebration of the presence of God in our midst; bringing us into communion with God and with one another; feeding and nourishing our souls. It also anticipates the day when we will eat and drink with Christ in his Father's kingdom.

The catechism highlights Christ's institution of this rite, which has a future orientation. It is to be celebrated with thankful remembrance of him and his saving work, made present through its administration such that participants experience enriching fellowship with God and with one another.

In summary, A Reforming Catholic Confession and the New City Catechism are two examples of *mere ecclesiology* approaches to the ordinances or sacraments that appeal to a broad evangelical audience.

More Ordinances or Sacraments

Working within this broad framework, I turn to a discussion of the beliefs and practices that distinguish particular churches with respect to the ordinances.

As noted by the New City Catechism, the first and most obvious difference is what name is given to these rites. For some churches, they are *sacraments*; for others, they are *ordinances*. The term *sacrament* is derived from the Latin word *sacramentum*, which was used in Latin translations of the Bible. The Greek New Testament uses the word *mystērion*, or "mystery," to refer to matters that God once hid but has now revealed through the gospel (e.g., Rom. 16:25–26; Eph. 3:3–13; Col. 1:24–27). The early church applied this term to its administration of baptism and the Lord's Supper, considering these ceremonies to reveal a mystery of divine grace. When the Greek Bible was translated into Latin, *mystērion* became *sacramentum*, which could refer to a rite or an oath of allegiance. By the fifth century, Augustine's definition became decisive for the church: a sacrament is an outward and visible sign of an inward and invisible grace.[5] The church considered these two rites sacred signs designed by God to indicate a divine reality, a reality that was included in and caused by the signs themselves. When the sacrament of baptism is administered to an adult or an infant, she becomes the recipient of divine grace. Similarly, when church members participate in the sacrament of Communion, they receive the grace of God.

The term *ordinance* became associated with these two rites when Protestant churches made a decisive break with the Roman Catholic Church. Included in the protest of some Protestants was a rejection of the word *sacrament*; it had too many connotations associated with the Catholic theology and practice of baptism and the Lord's Supper. In its place these Protestant churches put the term *ordinance*, signifying that these rites were ordained, or instituted, by Christ himself. He ordained baptism when he gave the Great Commission to his disciples (Matt. 28:18–20). As part of the church's discipleship of all the nations, it is to baptize in the name of the triune God. Jesus also ordained the Lord's Supper when he instituted it at his last supper with his disciples, shortly before his death (Matt. 26:26–29).

As for other points of variance, churches administer baptism differently because of divergent understandings of the recipients and nature of this sacrament, and they celebrate the Lord's Supper differently according to different names and understandings of its relationship to the presence of Jesus Christ. The details of these divergences are best discussed in relationship to each particular rite.

---

5. Augustine, *On the Catetchizing of the Uninstructed*, 26.50, in *Nicene and Post-Nicene Fathers of the Christian Church*, 1st ser., ed. Philip Schaff (1886–1890; repr., Peabody, MA: Hendrickson, 1994), 3:312.

Baptism

To avoid overemphasizing the differences to the neglect of the commonalities, I mention several points that unite churches regarding baptism.

Mere Baptism

Four more commonalities concerning baptism are its manner, nature, element, and timing. All churches administer Trinitarian baptism once only, as participants are baptized into the name of the Father and of the Son and of the Holy Spirit. This association with the triune God portrays the reality of salvation, as expressed in the Nicene-Constantinopolitan's affirmation "I confess one baptism for the forgiveness of sins." Though the quantity of the element used may vary, the element with which participants are baptized is water. Historically, baptism has been considered the initiatory rite of the church: before people may participate in the Lord's Supper, which is the ongoing rite of the church, they must first be baptized.

More Baptism

The major divergences with respect to baptism are due to different understandings of the recipients and nature of this sacrament. I begin with a brief history and then turn to the differences.[6]

In the early church, baptism by immersion was predominantly administered to people who grasped the gospel, repented of their sins, and believed in Jesus Christ for salvation (Acts 2:37–41), though some historians suggest that biblical evidence may support an early practice of infant baptism (Acts 2:38–39;

---

6. Much of the following discussion is taken from Gregg R. Allison, "The Ordinances of the Church," The Gospel Coalition, Concise Theology Series, https://www.thegospelcoalition.org/essay/the-ordinances-of-the-church/. Used by permission of the Gospel Coalition.

16:15, 33; 1 Cor. 1:16). An important development was the turn to the baptism of infants as the dominant form of baptism. Some leaders denounced the practice, while others traced its origin to the apostles. The church noted a parallel between the baptism of infants and the Old Testament rite of circumcision, as suggested by Paul (Col. 2:11–12). The church also linked infant baptism to the removal of original sin. By the fifth century, infant baptism became the official practice of the church.[7]

Today, the ordinance of baptism is administered to infants (*paedobaptism*; Gk. *pais, paid-*, "child") and to believing adults (*credobaptism*; Lat. *credo*, "I believe"). These two views of the recipients of baptism express different beliefs about its nature.

Paedobaptism. Discussion of the nature of paedobaptism falls under two categories. The first category is exemplified by Roman Catholicism. As the first of the seven Roman Catholic sacraments, baptism cleanses its recipients from original sin, regenerates them, and incorporates them into the Catholic Church. Effective *ex opere operato* (by administering the sacrament), baptism infuses grace and thereby begins the lifelong process of transforming the character of the Catholic faithful. Cooperating with this grace, Catholics become progressively more and more justified and, engaging in good works, are enabled to merit eternal life. Importantly, baptismal regeneration means that baptized infants are saved; indeed, this sacrament is necessary for salvation. No Protestant church embraces this Roman Catholic perspective on infant baptism.

The second category of infant baptism is exemplified by two branches of (historical) Protestantism: Lutheran and Reformed. Martin Luther championed infant baptism in a very

---

7. For further discussion of the historical development of baptism, see Gregg R. Allison, *Historical Theology: An Introduction to Christian Doctrine* (Grand Rapids, MI: Zondervan, 2011), chap. 28.

different way from Roman Catholic paedobaptism. Specifically, he linked it to the word of God and faith. Speaking of its benefits, Luther argued, "It works forgiveness of sins, delivers from death and the devil, and gives eternal salvation to all who believe, as the Word and promises of God declare."[8] Key to the administration of infant baptism is not the ceremony itself: "It is not the water . . . that does it, but the Word of God which is with and in the water, and faith, which trusts in the Word of God in the water. For without the Word of God the water is nothing but water, and no baptism; but with the Word of God it is baptism."[9] As for the aspect of faith, Luther affirmed, "Faith clings to the water, and believes that it is baptism, in which there is pure salvation and life; not [salvation] through the water . . . but through the fact that it is embodied in the Word and institution of God, and the name of God inheres in it."[10] How faith is possible in an infant was a question that Luther answered differently as his theology evolved over time.

For Reformed churches, baptism is a means of grace by which God offers a promise to its recipients: they will thereby become partakers of the salvation of which baptism is the divinely appointed sign and seal. By being baptized, infants are not saved. Rather, they are incorporated into the covenant community in which they will hear the gospel and, as heirs of the covenant promise, will embrace the grace of God by faith for salvation. Moreover, the sacrament is not effective *ex opere operato* but depends on the word and the Spirit for its validity.

John Calvin emphasized an analogy between circumcision, the sign of the old covenant, and baptism, the sign of the new

---

8. Martin Luther, *Small Catechism*, 4.2, in *Creeds of Christendom*, ed. Philip Schaff (New York: Harper, 1877), 3:85.

9. Luther, *Small Catechism*, 4.3, in Schaff, *Creeds of Christendom*, 3:86.

10. Martin Luther, "Of Infant Baptism," *Large Catechism*, 4:28, in *Triglot Concordia: The Symbolical Books of the Evangelical Lutheran Church*, trans. F. Bente and W. H. T. Dan (St. Louis, MO: Concordia, 1921), 739.

covenant. As circumcision marked the children of Israelites as different from the surrounding pagan nations, so baptism marks the children of Christians as different from unbelievers— indeed, as holy. Calvin highlighted two benefits of infant baptism, as I note elsewhere:

> For the parents, the benefit is seeing God's covenant of mercy being extended to their children. As for the benefit for the infants: "Being engrafted into the body of the church, they are somewhat more commended to the other members. Then, when they have grown up, they are greatly spurred to an earnest zeal for worshiping God, by whom they were received as children through a solemn symbol of adoption before they were old enough to recognize him as Father." Accordingly, "infants are baptized into future repentance and faith."[11]

Consequently, while there is a family resemblance between the practice of infant baptism by the Roman Catholic Church, Lutheran churches, and Reformed churches, the understanding of the nature of infant baptism differs significantly between these churches.

In addition to Lutheran and Reformed churches, others that baptize infants include Anglican churches, Episcopalian churches, Methodist churches, Congregationalist churches, Nazarene churches, and more.

Credobaptism. According to credobaptism, baptism is an ordinance instituted by Christ for people who offer a credible profession of faith in him and who, in obedience to his command, are baptized. Unlike previous types of baptism—for example,

---

11. Allison, *Historical Theology*, 630. The citations are from John Calvin, *Institutes of the Christian Religion*, ed. John T. McNeill, trans. Ford Lewis Battles, Library of Christian Classics (Louisville: Westminster, 1960), 4.16.9 (2:1332); 4.16.20 (2:1343).

proselyte baptism for Gentiles associating with the people of Israel, the baptism of John the Baptist—credobaptism is a new rite instituted for the new covenant church. In most cases, the mode of baptism is immersion: people are completely lowered under the water and brought up out of the water. Discussion of the nature of credobaptism falls under two categories. The first category is exemplified by Southern Baptists. According to the Baptist Faith and Message (2000), article 7, baptism "is an act of obedience symbolizing the believer's faith in a crucified, buried, and risen Savior, the believer's death to sin, the burial of the old life, and the resurrection to walk in newness of life in Christ Jesus." Accordingly, the nature of baptism is a human act by which faith in God's provision of salvation is expressed. It is not salvific but testifies to salvation already experienced.

The second category builds on this common view of the nature of baptism by expanding on its meanings, as indicated in the New Testament, in the following ways:

1. On the basis of Jesus's command to baptize "in the name of the Father and of the Son and of the Holy Spirit" (Matt. 28:19), baptism associates new believers with the triune God.

2. As noted above, baptism by immersion vividly portrays new believers' identification with the death, burial, and resurrection of Christ (Rom. 6:3–5; Gal. 3:26–28).

3. Baptism signifies cleansing from sin, in accordance with Peter's Pentecost message: "Repent and be baptized every one of you, in the name of Jesus Christ for the forgiveness of your sins" (Acts 2:38; cf. Ezek. 36:25; Acts 22:16).

4. Escape from divine judgment is pictured in baptism. Just as Noah and his family escaped God's judgment of the flood (the antitype), so also Christians escape divine

judgment via baptism—the plunging under water as a type of death (1 Pet. 3:20–21).

5. Baptism symbolizes incorporation into the church. It is the initiatory rite, signaling new believers' intention to follow obediently and faithfully the mediator of the new covenant, Jesus Christ, in new covenant community.[12]

Accordingly, whether believer's baptism is practiced with a more limited or more expansive understanding of the nature of baptism, it is administered not to infants but only to those who can offer a credible profession of faith.

In summary, my discussion has treated both *mere baptism* and *more baptism*. This ordinance or sacrament has commonalities shared by all churches and important divergences distinguishing churches. These differences—paedobaptism and credobaptism—are particularly due to disagreements concerning the recipients and the nature of baptism.

Lord's Supper, Eucharist, Communion, or Breaking of Bread

Again, to avoid overemphasizing the differences to the neglect of the commonalities, I mention several more points that unite churches in regard to this rite. For simplicity's sake, I use the term *Communion* in the titles of this section.

Mere Communion

Three more commonalities are the regularity, the elements, and the timing of Communion. All churches administer it on a regular basis, be that weekly, monthly, quarterly, or annually. The elements with which this ordinance is administered are bread and the fruit of the vine, which for most churches is wine but

---

12. For further discussion of the various meanings of baptism, see Gregg R. Allison, *Sojourners and Strangers: The Doctrine of the Church*, Foundations of Evangelical Theology (Wheaton, IL: Crossway, 2012), 353–57.

for some is grape juice. In relation to baptism, which is the initiatory rite of the church, Communion is the ongoing rite that can be received only after one has been baptized.

More Communion

The divergences with respect to this sacrament have to do with the different names for it and the different understandings of its relationship to the presence of Jesus Christ. I begin with the diversity of names, briefly sketch the historical development, then turn to the differences regarding Christ's presence.[13]

This ordinance is referred to by various names. It is *the Lord's Supper* because Jesus instituted it as part of his last supper with his disciples shortly before his crucifixion. An important part of that inaugural celebration was the future prospect of Jesus once again enjoying it with his church after his return, an eschatological event known as the marriage supper of the Lamb (Rev. 19:9). This ordinance is also referred to as *(Holy) Communion* because as church members participate in it, they experience—that is, enjoy communion with—the blood and body of Jesus Christ (1 Cor. 10:16–17). Many churches call this sacrament *the Eucharist*, which is a transliteration of the Greek word *eucharistia*, or "thanksgiving." As Jesus instituted this rite, "he took bread, and *when he had given thanks*, he broke it and gave it to them, saying, 'This is my body, which is given for you. Do this in remembrance of me'" (Luke 22:19). Likewise, "he took a cup, and *when he had given thanks* he gave it to them, saying, 'Drink of it, all of you, for this is my blood of the covenant, which is poured out for many for the forgiveness of sins'" (Matt. 26:27–28). Thus, *Eucharist* underscores this

---

13. Much of the following discussion is taken from Gregg R. Allison, "The Ordinances of the Church," The Gospel Coalition, Concise Theology Series, https://www.thegospelcoalition.org/essay/the-ordinances-of-the-church/. Used by permission of the Gospel Coalition.

aspect of thanksgiving. Some churches refer to this ordinance as *breaking of bread*, which, as we just saw, was the first symbolic action in which Jesus engaged as he inaugurated the rite (Matt. 26:26; cf. 1 Cor. 11:24). The expression *breaking of bread* in two Acts narratives (2:42; 20:7) may also refer to this rite.

In the early church, only baptized believers in proper relationship to Christ could participate in this ordinance, which was celebrated weekly. In terms of the meaning of the Lord's Supper, the early church held several views. Some saw it as a sacrifice, linked to the prophecy of Malachi (Mal. 1:10–11). As to the nature of this sacrifice, some believed that the sacrifices are the bread and wine as fruits of divine creation, while others held that the sacrifices are the actual body and blood of Christ. Others focused on the Lord's Supper as an act of commemoration. Still others considered it in strongly symbolic terms. The early church also underscored several benefits of participation in the Lord's Supper, including release from death, nourishment, and sanctification. Eventually, four positions on the nature of the Lord's Supper developed, all of which continue to be held today.[14]

Transubstantiation. Transubstantiation is the Roman Catholic position, officially proclaimed in 1215. During the administration of the sacrament of the Eucharist, the bread is transubstantiated—or changed—into the body of Christ, and the wine into the blood of Christ, by the power of God. As explained by Thomas Aquinas, transubstantiation is the change (Lat. *trans*) of *substance* (that which makes something what it is). The *accidents* (the characteristics that can be perceived by the senses), however, remain the same. As the sacrament of the Eucharist is administered, though the bread still looks, smells, feels, and

---

14. For further discussion of the historical development of Communion, see Allison, *Historical Theology*, chap. 29.

tastes like bread, its substance has been changed into the body of Christ. Similarly, though the wine still looks, smells, and tastes like wine, its substance has been changed into the blood of Christ. By participating in the Eucharist, the Catholic faithful receive an infusion of grace that transforms them, thereby enabling them to engage in good works and thus merit eternal life. All Protestant churches reject transubstantiation.

Consubstantiation (or sacramental union). Consubstantiation, or sacramental union, is the Lutheran view. As developed by Martin Luther, the Lord's Supper was a last testament made by Christ as he was about to die. In this promise he designated an inheritance—the forgiveness of sins—and appointed its heirs—all those who believe in his promise. Moreover, during the administration of the sacrament, Christ is truly present in both his deity and humanity, "in, with, and under" the substance of the bread and wine. Because Christ's body is everywhere present, and in accordance with his words of institution ("This is my body," Matt. 26:26), God brings about the presence of Christ in the Lord's Supper.

This view is not transubstantiation, for the elements do not undergo a change in substance. Rather, the presence of Christ is rendered in, with, and under the Communion elements. If we think of a sponge saturated with water, wherever the sponge is, there is the water, and wherever the water is, there is the sponge. But the sponge is not the water, nor is the water the sponge. In an analogous manner, where the bread and wine are, so too are the body and blood of Christ during the celebration of this rite.

Memorialism. Memorialism is the view of many nonsacramentalist (e.g., Baptist) churches. As developed by Huldrych Zwingli, this position holds that the Lord's Supper is a memorial of Christ's death. Being located in heaven, Christ's body and blood cannot be present in the ordinance. Moreover, Christ's words of institution—"This is my body" (Matt. 26:26)—are figurative and cannot be taken literally. Accordingly, the memorial view stands against both transubstantiation and consubstantiation. Most importantly, Jesus commanded, "Do this in remembrance of me" (Luke 22:19; 1 Cor. 11:24). Thus, the Lord's Supper is a memorial celebration by which the church remembers what Christ did on the cross to accomplish salvation. Picking up on Jesus's command, Paul instructed,

> For I received from the Lord what I also delivered to you, that the Lord Jesus on the night when he was betrayed took bread, and when he had given thanks, he broke it, and said, "This is my body, which is for you. Do this in remembrance of me." In the same way also he took the cup, after supper, saying, "This cup is the new covenant in my blood. Do this, as often as you drink it, in remembrance of me." For as often as you eat this bread and drink the cup, you proclaim the Lord's death until he comes. (1 Cor. 11:23–26)

The administration of the Lord's Supper, as a nonverbal but vivid portrayal of Christ's sacrificial death on the cross, prompts participants to recall that work and celebrate salvation.

Spiritual presence. Spiritual presence is the view of many Reformed Protestant churches (e.g., Presbyterian, Christian Reformed, Reformed Anglican, Reformed Baptist). Moving beyond the memorial view, John Calvin maintained that the bread and wine are certainly symbols, but they are not empty symbols. Indeed, they render what they symbolize. By his spiritual presence, Christ presents himself and his saving benefits through these means of grace. How Christ can be located in heaven and spiritually present in the Lord's Supper is ultimately a mystery. But Calvin invoked the power of the Holy Spirit to unite Christ in heaven with the church on earth. The benefits of this sacrament include participation with Christ, church unity, and nourishment toward sanctification.

Paul draws attention to this communion or fellowship with Christ: "The cup of blessing that we bless, is it not a participation in the blood of Christ? The bread that we break, is it not a participation in the body of Christ?" (1 Cor. 10:16). Neither transubstantiation nor consubstantiation, yet more than memorialism, the spiritual presence view underscores the particular manifestation of Christ and his saving benefits. As the one whose blood was shed and whose body was broken for our salvation, Christ is spiritually present to bless those who participate in him through this rite.

In summary, my discussion has treated both *mere Communion* and *more Communion*. This sacrament has commonalities shared by all churches and important divergences distinguishing churches. One difference—the name of this rite—is due to a particular focus on one aspect of the celebration: it is the Lord's Supper; Communion with Christ; the Eucharist, because thanksgiving is expressed for Christ's saving work; or breaking of bread, a key action during its administration. The other difference is due to disagreements concerning the presence of Christ as the rite is celebrated.

To conclude, I have treated the topic of the church's rites in terms of both *mere ordinances or sacraments*—what all churches believe about and practice in relation to baptism and Communion—and *more ordinances or sacraments*. *More baptism* addressed paedobaptism and credobaptism. *More Communion* discussed the differences between transubstantiation, consubstantiation (or sacramental union), memorialism, and spiritual presence.

7

The Ministries of the Church

Over the course of its two-thousand-year history, the church has engaged in ministry. Indeed, Christians and non-Christians alike, when asked what the church is, often identify it with activities like the Sunday morning worship service, catechism classes and Bible studies, proclamation of the gospel both locally and globally, and food pantries and medical clinics. Mission statements that capture the essence of these ministries abound:

- "Win, build, send."
- "Reach up, reach in, reach out."
- "Turn the inside out to draw the outside in."

These mottos summarize the commonalities of church ministry. Particular churches engage in actual ministry in distinct ways, especially when it comes to who exercises which roles in ministry and which gifts of the Spirit operate in ministry.

This chapter addresses the ministries of the church in terms of both *mere ministries*—what all churches believe about and practice in relation to them—and *more ministries*, with particular attention to the roles of men and women in ministry and whether the so-called "sign" or "miraculous" spiritual gifts continue in the church today.

Mere Ministries

All churches engage in the ministries that Scripture prescribes for their maturity and multiplication. According to a popular systematic theology, we "understand the purposes of the church in terms of ministry to God, ministry to believers, and ministry to the world."[1] This threefold orientation encapsulates the ways that many churches engage in ministry.

Ministry to God

As for ministry that is oriented toward God, "the church's purpose is to worship him,"[2] as portrayed in this vision of heavenly adoration:

> But you have come to Mount Zion and to the city of the living God, the heavenly Jerusalem, and to innumerable angels in festal gathering, and to the assembly of the firstborn who are enrolled in heaven, and to God, the judge of all, and to the spirits of the righteous made perfect, and to Jesus, the mediator of a new covenant, and to the sprinkled blood. (Heb. 12:22–24)

The church engages in such ministry toward God as its members gather regularly for the Sunday morning worship service. But this element is not reserved for this meeting. Rather, worship should be an important, even central, component of community-group gatherings, prayer summits, Sunday

---

1. Wayne Grudem, *Systematic Theology: An Introduction to Biblical Doctrine* (Grand Rapids, MI: Zondervan, 2004), 867.
2. Grudem, *Systematic Theology*, 867.

school classes, leadership-team meetings, kids' ministries, and more.

Ministry to Members

In terms of ministry toward its members, "the church has an obligation to nurture those who are already believers and build them up to maturity in the faith."[3] Indeed, Christ's gift of gifted leaders is "to equip the saints for the work of ministry, for building up the body of Christ, until we all attain to the unity of the faith and of the knowledge of the Son of God, to mature manhood, to the measure of the stature of the fullness of Christ" (Eph. 4:12–13). Through ministries of discipleship, one-on-one or small-group mentoring, community groups, men's and women's Bible studies, leadership training, and much more, this purpose of the church is actualized.

Ministry to the World

Ministry directed toward the world is twofold. Evangelism consists of proclaiming the gospel to unbelievers and living as stellar examples of Christlikeness so that they embrace Christ and become incorporated into the church. This aspect flows from Jesus's Great Commission to "make disciples of all nations" (Matt. 28:19). Ministry of mercy involves caring for the poor, orphans and widows, the disenfranchised, the elderly, and more, as Jesus instructed: "But love your enemies, and do good, and lend, expecting nothing in return, and your reward will be great, and you will be sons of the Most High, for he is kind to the ungrateful and the evil. Be merciful, even as your Father is merciful" (Luke 6:35–36). "Most importantly," as I state elsewhere,

---

3. Grudem, *Systematic Theology*, 867.

the church's responsibility to engage the world with particular concern to care for the poor and marginalized may be viewed as flowing from its embrace of the good news of Jesus Christ. That is, no disjuncture is promoted or permitted between the uniquely Christian responsibilities to connect missionally with the world and the general responsibilities to build civilization and stand against its dark side. . . . The gospel and compassionate assistance go together.[4]

Thus, as the church hosts medical clinics for immigrants without insurance and as its members provide practical assistance for widows in the neighborhood, such ministries flow from and engage unbelievers with the gospel.

The church does well to develop all three of these ministries. To focus on one or two at the expense of all three results in an unbalanced and limited church. Moreover, given the headship of Jesus Christ, the church must constantly ask itself a crucial question: What is the will of the Lord for our church in terms of its worship, nurture, and missional engagement? Tried and true programs should be evaluated for their fruitfulness. To rest on the motto "We've always done it this way" may spell obsolescence; tens of thousands of churches that rally around that motto are either in steep decline or dead. Indeed, as difficult as it may be, the church must learn how to contextualize its three ministries. Contextualization does not mean compromise, but it does mean embodying worship, discipleship, and mission in language and forms that communicate and exhibit the gospel in an intelligible way. As Timothy Keller observes, such sound contextualization "avoids making the message unnecessarily

---

4. Gregg R. Allison, *Sojourners and Strangers: The Doctrine of the Church*, Foundations of Evangelical Theology (Wheaton, IL: Crossway, 2012), 462.

alien to that culture, yet without removing or obscuring the scandal and offense of biblical truth."[5]

Spiritual Gifts for Ministry

To guide and empower the church for its engagement in these three ministries, the Holy Spirit provides gifts. Specifically, "to each [church member] is given the manifestation of the Spirit for the common good" (1 Cor. 12:7). Key to this point is the dual dimensionality of such gifts. One side is the divine dimension. Empowered by the same Spirit who sovereignly distributes them (1 Cor. 12:11), spiritual gifts foster worship of God, nurturing of church members, and connecting missionally with unbelievers and those in need. On the other side is the human dimension. Exercised in an atmosphere of love (1 Cor. 13), gifts are given to and employed by church members. I note elsewhere,

> As the gospel is announced, it is the evangelist who proclaims it. As a meeting is directed, it is guided by one who has the gift of leadership. As comfort is extended, one with the gift of mercy is ministering. As a revelation is communicated, it is spoken by a prophet. That is, the exercise of the gifts is fully (though not merely) human activity "for the common good."[6]

Still, evangelism, leadership, mercy, teaching, and other activities are not restricted to certain members who have such gifts. Certainly, all members are called to share the good news, teach and admonish one another (Col. 3:16), show hospitality, give sacrificially, and the like. But the Spirit's particular gifting, and the Spirit-empowered deployment of spiritual gifts

---

5. Timothy Keller, *Center Church: Doing Balanced, Gospel-Centered Ministry in Your City* (Grand Rapids, MI: Zondervan, 2012), 89.

6. Allison, *Sojourners and Strangers*, 470.

by members, undergirds the ministry of the church in the way that Scripture envisions. Indeed, in another place I explain,

> First and foremost, and as a foundation for the second dimension, a divine dimension is at work: Christ himself, as the head of the church who unites each part together, "makes the body grow" (Eph. 4:16); thus, it "grows with a growth that is from God" (Col. 2:19). Second and derivatively, from this divine foundation, a human dimension is at work: the whole church, and each and every one of its parts, equipped with everything it needs for growth, must build itself up in love (Eph. 4:16).[7]

This is the dual dimensionality of spiritual gifts.

In four of its passages, the New Testament provides lists of spiritual gifts. Consolidating the lists, the gifts or gifted people include the following:

- apostles
- prophets or prophecy
- teachers, teaching, or shepherd-teachers
- evangelists
- words of wisdom
- words of knowledge
- exhortation
- leading or administration
- faith
- service or helping
- giving
- acts of mercy
- gifts of healing
- miracles or working of miracles
- distinguishing of spirits

---

7. Allison, *Sojourners and Strangers*, 470–71.

- kinds of tongues or speaking in tongues
- interpretation of tongues

Other "gifts" may include these:

- craftsmanship (Ex. 31:3; 35:31)
- artistic abilities and creativity
- marriage and its counterpart, singleness (1 Cor. 7:7)

Below we discuss which gifts continue to be distributed today by the Holy Spirit and thus are operative in the church. Importantly for our *mere ministry* presentation, the majority of the gifts just itemized form a consensus list, and all churches agree that the Spirit continues to allocate the spiritual gifts of teaching, evangelism, exhortation, leading, faith, helps, distinguishing of spirits, giving, and mercy. Accordingly, *mere ministry* embraces these gifts and the Spirit's empowerment of them, resulting in the dual dimensionality of spiritual gifts for ministry to God, ministry to church members, and ministry to the world.

The church does well to help its members identify their gift or gifts. This help may come from a spiritual-gift inventory, a tool by which members discover their interest in, experience with, and passion for various ministries. These tendencies are compiled and then connected with a gift or gifts, and members are encouraged to consider that to be their gift or gifts. Other people who know the members well may be enlisted to confirm or question the results.

While not as "objective" and formal as a spiritual-gift inventory, an important help is offered when church members speak words of encouragement to other members who teach fruitfully, help well, give sacrificially, pray effectively for healing, prophesy accurately, and more. For example, someone might say, "I was blessed by the consensus you achieved when you led that meeting. You demonstrated a fine ability to encourage everyone to talk and to bring harmony out of many disparate voices.

Have you considered that you may have the gift of leadership?" Furthermore, it is often the case that people discover their gift or gifts as they engage in ministry. So the church does well to involve all its members in ministry and pray to discover the giftings distributed and empowered by the Spirit.

Having identified their gift or gifts, members need to be trained how to exercise that gift or set of gifts. Teachers can be taught how to teach more clearly and passionately. Leaders can be trained to lead more effectively and humbly. Merciful people can be instructed how to express their compassion and care in ways that don't lead to burnout and that don't stir up false hope. Prophets can be coached how to communicate their prophecies more discerningly and appropriately.

Having identified and been prepared to use their spiritual gift or gifts, members should be launched into ministries that call for the use of their gift or gifts. Teachers should teach Sunday school. Leaders should lead elder meetings. Healers should pray for healing. Administrators should be responsible for budgetary matters. Evangelists should share the gospel regularly. Prophetesses should communicate their prophecies in an orderly manner and for evaluation.

Spiritually gifted people engaging with their gifts in the proper ministries foster the church's growth and multiplication in worship, discipleship, and mission.

More Ministries

All churches affirm and involve themselves in ministries to God, members, and the world, and they minister through the gifting and empowerment of the Holy Spirit. At the same time, churches differ in their understanding of the roles of men and women in ministries and the types of gifts that the Spirit distributes and energizes today. I turn now to a discussion of *more ministries*.

More Roles in Ministry

Who exercises which roles in ministry? I focus on the two "official" ministries of the church, the eldership/pastorate and the diaconate. May both men and women minister as elders/pastors of the church, thereby teaching, leading, praying, and shepherding? May both men and women minister as deacons and deaconesses of the church, thereby being leading servants?

Eldership/Pastorate

With notable consistency, the church in different eras (early church, Middle Ages, Reformation and post-Reformation period, and the majority of the modern era) and in many and vastly different contexts and cultures (Middle East, North Africa, Europe, Americas, Asia) has with rare exception chosen only qualified men as its bishops, elders, pastors, or overseers. The church has often justified this exclusive choice on biblical passages (e.g., 1 Cor. 14:33–35; 1 Tim. 2:12–3:7) and theological grounds (e.g., male leadership in the church should reflect male leadership in the home).

It could be argued that other factors played a role in this as well. One cultural factor is patriarchalism: the church, existing in a social system that was controlled by men, was led by men only. Another cultural factor is paternalism: men in the church viewed women as inherently inferior, more susceptible to deception, weaker spiritually, and prone to becoming sources of temptation; therefore, they limited women from involvement in ministry. An additional cultural factor is an absence of opportunities for women owing to a restriction on their education, access to finances, and more. Very darkly, misogyny has exacerbated this situation. An ecclesial reason for the restriction of women in ministry is the Roman Catholic Church's reservation of the priesthood for men. Its reasoning: when Jesus chose his twelve apostles, he selected men only. Moreover, priests act in the person of Christ, so as he is male, they too must be male. While not grounding the issue in the same way as Catholics, some Protestant churches have been characterized by an unquestioned or unchastened tradition in this matter.

Overall, women have been significantly restricted in terms of the ministries in which they may be involved.

In the last fifty years, this traditional consensus has come under close scrutiny and begun to unravel. Today, a key debate rages between two positions on women in ministry. To be clear, the issue is not whether women are to be involved in ministry. Everyone agrees that women share the gospel, disciple believers in fulfillment of the Great Commission, teach (e.g., Col. 3:16; Titus 2:3–5), show mercy to the poor and disenfranchised, pray, and much more. Rather, the issue has to do with the scope of women's ministries. One view is complementarianism, while the other is egalitarianism. I present each position in turn.

Complementarianism. Complementarianism is the view that men and women are complementary or correspond to one another, filling out and completing one another. Complementarity features two important aspects. Men and women are equal in three principal ways: being created in the image of God, enjoying access to salvation through Jesus Christ, and receiving the gifts of the Holy Spirit. That is, men and women alike bear the divine image. Men and women alike may be rescued from sin by Christ and, united together, be incorporated into his body. And men and women alike receive the full range of spiritual gifts; that is, there are no gender-specific gifts. At the same time, men and women are different in relationships and roles. Such distinctions may appear in several realms. With respect to the home, husbands lead, and their wives submit to them. In the church, elder/pastor responsibilities are reserved for qualified men. Women, while participating in many ministries, may not hold the office of elder/pastor. These distinctions come in various combinations. By contrast, egalitarianism denies some or all distinctions.

Because this book treats ecclesiology, I focus my attention on distinctions between men and women in the church. The key passage that places restrictions on women in ministry is 1 Timothy 2:11–14:

> Let a woman learn quietly with all submissiveness. I do not permit a woman to teach or to exercise authority over a man; rather, she is to remain quiet. For Adam was formed first, then Eve; and Adam was not deceived, but the woman was deceived and became a transgressor.

The traditional interpretation goes like this: "The apostle's instructions are framed by two comments about a woman's conduct: she is to learn submissively and, rather than teach or exercise authority, she is to remain quiet."[8] Paul next articulates two prohibitions about a woman teaching and exercising authority. Diagrammatically,

I do not permit [women in the church]
　to teach [the positive communication of biblical truth
　　and sound doctrine]
　　or
　to exercise authority [the positive role of proper
　　church leadership]
　　but
　to remain quiet [the positive posture for learning and
　　submitting]

Paul considers these two activities of teaching and exercising authority to be positive in and of themselves. He prohibits women, however, from exercising these good ministries for two reasons

---

8. Allison, *Sojourners and Strangers*, 225.

that appear next in the text. The first reason appeals to the order of creation: Adam's creation preceded Eve's (1 Tim. 2:13). Alluding to the creation account in Genesis 2, Paul underscores the flow of the narrative: God first creates Adam (Gen. 2:7), and then God creates Eve (Gen. 2:18–25). This creational order is significant for the prohibition of women teaching and exercising authority. The second reason is the nature of Eve's fall into sin: Eve was deceived by Satan and thus sinned, whereas Adam was not so deceived (1 Tim. 2:14). Alluding to the account of the fall in Genesis 3, Paul underscores that Eve was tricked by the serpent into violating God's prohibition not to eat of the fruit of the tree of the knowledge of good and evil (Gen. 3:1–7). Because of the type of Eve's sin, or as punishment for her sin through deceit, women are prohibited from teaching and exercising authority. A more complete diagram:

I do not permit [women in the church]
    to teach [the positive communication of biblical truth
        and sound doctrine]
        or
    to exercise authority [the positive role of proper
        church leadership]
        but
    to remain quiet [the positive posture of submissiveness
        in learning and obeying]
for two reasons [from the narratives of Gen. 2–3]
    the order of creation
    the sin of Eve

Thus, women in the church are not allowed to teach but should learn quietly, and they are not to exercise authority but to obey submissively.

Paul's directives raise two important questions: From whom are women to learn? And to whom are women to submit? If we continue reading Paul's letter, we have his answers (1 Tim.

3:1–7): Women are to learn from the elders/pastors, who bear the responsibility to teach. This application is also true for all nonelder men. And women are to submit to the elders/pastors, who have the duty to lead the church. This application is also true for all nonelder men. Both points underscore the positive posture of learning from and submitting to church leaders. As I summarize this view elsewhere,

> In the assembly, when men and women gather together to worship, the Lord himself has appointed pastors for the church, and two of their primary activities are communicating sound biblical and theological truth and exercising authority as leaders responsible for the church. They must be qualified *men*, not *women*.[9]

Egalitarianism. Egalitarianism is the position that men and women are equal to one another in nature, relationships, and roles. In agreement with complementarianism, this view embraces the great equalities of men and women alike bearing the divine image, being redeemed through Christ and incorporated into his body, and receiving the full range of spiritual gifts. In contrast to complementarianism, egalitarianism adds equalities in other realms. With respect to the home, husbands and wives share equal authority and submit to each other. In the church, qualified men and qualified women may hold the office of elder/pastor. Moreover, these equalities come in various combinations. Egalitarianism stands in contrast to complementarianism, which believes men and women to be equal in nature yet distinct in relationships and roles.

Because this book treats ecclesiology, I focus my attention on the equality between men and women in the church. The key passage that emphasizes this equal status and role is Galatians 3:26–28:

---

9. Allison, *Sojourners and Strangers*, 227–28; italics original.

In Christ Jesus you are all sons of God, through faith. For as many of you as were baptized into Christ have put on Christ. There is neither Jew nor Greek, there is neither slave nor free, there is no male and female, for you are all one in Christ Jesus.

A common egalitarian interpretation goes like this: Unlike the old covenant for the Jewish people, with its emphasis on inequality between men and women, the new covenant for the church highlights the equality of men and women. Moreover, such equality pertains not only to their salvation through Christ; it also means that both men and women share "equal opportunity to participate in the spiritual and religious life of the community."[10] Practically speaking, both men and women alike may hold the office of elder/pastor, as the church cannot make any distinction for the officeholders on the basis of gender.

But why should this passage take precedence over other biblical texts that present distinctions between men and women in their roles in the church? Many egalitarians maintain that it offers a universal perspective on this topic while the other passages (such as 1 Tim. 2:11–14) reflect very limited first-century perspectives that are culturally influenced. The church is to adhere to and actualize the universal view and ignore the narrow culturally determined views. Additionally, Galatians 3:26–28 affirms spiritual equality between men and women, and this affirmation cannot be squared with the complementarian position that men possess spiritual authority over women, who are to be submissive to them.

Egalitarianism dissents from the complementarian interpretation of 1 Timothy 2:11–14 and offers various alternative understandings. As I have pointed out elsewhere, some proponents of egalitarianism focus on

---

10. Rebecca Merrill Groothuis, *Good News for Women: A Biblical Picture of Gender Equality* (Grand Rapids, MI: Baker, 1997), 35.

the lack of education for women in the first century; given this context, the apostle Paul denied them the responsibility to teach and exercise authority in the church. . . . Once this cultural context changes—that is, once women have access to education and become well equipped for this responsibility, as they may be today—they may indeed teach and exercise authority in the church.[11]

Other proponents reconstruct the cultural context that called forth Paul's prohibition of women from teaching and exercising authority. Certain women in the Ephesian church were provoking disruptive worship by teaching in an oppressive manner so as to gain advantage over the men. Perplexed and frustrated by this disorderly atmosphere, the men became angry with and quarrelsome toward the women. To put a halt to this corrosive situation, Paul prohibited the women from engaging in ministry.

Still other egalitarians understand the two activities that the apostle forbids to be the negative endeavors of teaching heresy and usurping authority or exercising it in a domineering way. Diagrammatically,

I do not permit [women in the church]
> to teach [the negative communication of poor biblical interpretation and false doctrine]
>> *or*
> to exercise authority [the negative role of usurped church leadership or domineering leadership]
>> *but*
> to remain quiet [the negative posture as punishment for wrong conduct]

As to be expected, Paul views negatively these two activities of teaching heresy and exercising usurped or domineering

---

11. Allison, *Sojourners and Strangers*, 230–31.

authority. Accordingly, he prohibits women from engaging in ministries that are evil or wrong in themselves. Once the nature of their ministry changes, however, women may indeed teach biblical truth and sound doctrine and exercise proper leadership in the church.

My view is that the complementarian position is the stronger of the two positions. It makes better sense of the structure and argument of 1 Timothy 2:11–14 without appealing to a complicated and quite speculative reconstruction of the background situation. The complementarian position roots Paul's prohibitions not in cultural reasons—for example, the lack of education for women in the early church—but in the order of creation and the fall of Eve. These are the apostle's transcultural reasons for his limitations on women teaching and leading the church.

Additionally, the complementarian position views the ministries of teaching and exercising authority as positive activities rather than as negative ones. Throughout his pastoral letters (1 and 2 Timothy and Titus), Paul applauds and promotes teaching. For example, he lists teaching as one of the competencies of elders/pastors (1 Tim. 3:2) and singles out for commendation those leaders who give themselves to teaching (1 Tim. 5:17). He urges Timothy to teach sound doctrine (1 Tim. 4:11, 13; 5:7; 6:3). He enjoins older women to teach younger women (Titus 2:3–5). Paul holds teaching in high esteem. Moreover, had he wanted to prohibit women from teaching heresy, he certainly could have done so, as he warns against teaching "different [i.e., false] doctrine" at the beginning of his first letter to Timothy (1 Tim. 1:3). Likewise, Paul approves authoritative leadership, again as exemplified by elders/pastors (1 Tim. 3:4–5; 5:17). As I explain elsewhere,

> Ultimately, the egalitarian position views this section of Scripture negatively. Paul's prohibition is considered to be

a reactive ban directed at a sinful situation, with reasons for the proscription viewed as corrective in nature. But why does one assume that such a prohibition is negative, or seek to reconstruct the background situation in such a way as to justify this negative viewpoint? Why is it not considered as a means of promoting propriety for the church?[12]

Moreover, Galatians 3:26–28 is not so much about equality as it is about unity between men and women, who are all one now that they are in Christ. Certainly, they are equal in Christ, equal in having access to salvation, equal in terms of experiencing forgiveness of sins, equal with respect to enjoying eternal life. But such equality does not mean that men and women are the same with regard to other matters, like roles in the church, which are not at all in view in this passage. Similarly, the fact that men and women alike are recipients of the full range of spiritual gifts—there are no gender-specific gifts—and are empowered by the Spirit to use their gifts does not stand over the Spirit-breathed biblical texts that prohibit women from holding the office of elder/pastor.

Importantly, proponents of egalitarianism highlight the valued ministries of women in the early church. The list includes the diaconate ministry of women (exemplified by Phoebe, Rom. 16:1–2), the eyewitness testimony of women to the resurrection of Jesus (Matt. 28:1–10), the prayerful participation of women in the upper room prior to the descent of the Holy Spirit (Acts 1:13–14), women's reception and exercise of the gifts of the outpoured Spirit (Acts 2:16–18; exemplified by the four prophetesses, Acts 21:8–9), the association of women with the apostles (exemplified by Junia[s], Rom. 16:7, and by Euodia and Syntyche, Phil. 4:2–3), women praying and prophesying in

---

12. Allison, *Sojourners and Strangers*, 237.

the church (1 Cor. 11:5), women's corrective training of church leaders (exemplified by Priscilla, Acts 18:26), and women hosting house churches (exemplified by Lydia, Acts 16:13–15, 40, and by Nympha, Col. 4:15). Such examples find counterparts in women whose important roles are set forth in the Old Testament (e.g., Sarah, Deborah, Ruth, Hannah, Esther, and the model wife in Prov. 31).

Focusing on the New Testament, there are stellar examples of women playing crucial roles in the early church. Egalitarian proponents apply these examples in support of their call for the equality of women and men to hold the office of elder/pastor. Complementarian proponents embrace these examples yet draw a different conclusion: "Involvement in these important activities is one matter; incorporation of women as elders of a church is another matter, and biblical evidence for the former does not translate into evidence for the latter."[13]

Contemporary complementarianism. Among other things, noting the list of women's roles in ministry has prompted some complementarians to reexamine their application—though not interpretation—of biblical passages such as 1 Timothy 2:11–14. Indeed, contemporary discussion of women's roles has led to a spectrum of applications, which I summarize briefly.

Minimum complementarianism. In agreement with all forms of complementarianism, minimum complementarianism maintains that women may not hold the office of elder/pastor. Still, qualified women may occasionally preach—for example, deliver the Sunday morning sermon. They may exhort—for example, on Mother's Day present a message to mothers in the congregation immediately after the sermon. They may preside over the worship service—for example, oversee the administra-

---

13. Allison, *Sojourners and Strangers*, 238.

tion of baptism and the Lord's Supper. They may teach on any topic in mixed-gender settings—for example, teach Galatians to an adult Sunday school class (with both men and women present) or teach the doctrine of the Trinity in a theology class. Moreover, qualified women may hold the office of deaconess.

To focus on one aspect, how could women teach as part of the Sunday morning worship service? Some proponents of minimum complementarianism support their view with an interpretation of 1 Timothy 2:12 that takes Paul's prohibition to refer to women teaching with authority. To paraphrase the first part of this verse, Paul urges, "I do not permit a woman to teach with authority over a man." That is, women may not teach with the authority of the church; only elders have this responsibility, and women cannot be elders. And women may not transmit the official, authoritative doctrine of the church and other teaching that binds the conscience of its members. The elders, however, may permit a woman to teach under their authority (and it should be clear that she is doing so) but not in an authoritative way and not on a topic that is authoritative teaching.[14]

Moderate complementarianism. Like all forms of complementarianism, moderate complementarianism maintains that women may not hold the office of elder/pastor. Specifically, they may not preach, exhort, or preside over the worship service. But they may plan and play a prominent role in the liturgy—for example, be the main singer, lead responsive readings, pray, and read Scripture. In mixed-gender adult settings, they may not teach on topics mostly focused on Bible exposition and theology but may teach on other topics such as missions, mercy ministries, and counseling. Moreover, qualified women may hold the office of deaconess.

---

14. My thanks to Brandon Shields and Todd Engstrom for offering perspective on this question.

Some proponents of moderate complementarianism support their position by appealing to Paul's instructions to a woman "who prays or prophesies" in the worship service (1 Cor. 11:4–5). Clearly, it is proper for women to engage in public praying. Moreover, if prophecy is the spontaneous reception and communication of a divine revelation, and women engage in prophecy, it is surely proper for women to read written Scripture in the public worship service. Furthermore, Paul prohibits women from teaching sound doctrine and exercising authority at the highest level—both duties are the responsibility of the elders/pastors. Therefore, the church should guard against illegitimately prohibiting women from engaging in teaching and leading activities that are not elder-level duties.

Maximum complementarianism. Similar to all forms of complementarianism, maximum complementarianism maintains that women may not hold the office of elder/pastor. Moreover, they may not serve in any public ministry that is a mixed-gender adult setting; rather, they are to focus their ministries on women and children. Commonly, churches characterized by this position have only the office of deacon, which is reserved for qualified men. In such structures, the issue of deaconesses is moot. Some churches that distinguish between eldership/pastorate and diaconate may still restrict women from being deaconesses. Other churches permit women to serve in this office.

Some proponents of maximum complementarianism support their position by appealing to Paul's instructions in 1 Corinthians 14:33–35:

> As in all the churches of the saints, the women should keep silent in the churches. For they are not permitted to speak, but should be in submission, as the Law also says. If there is anything they desire to learn, let them ask

their husbands at home. For it is shameful for a woman to speak in church.

The all-encompassing nature of Paul's prohibition of women speaking in church is clear: his ban is to be observed in all the churches. It is supported by an appeal to "the Law," which some take to be a summary reference to the perspective of the entirety of the Old Testament. And women have a ready provision for learning about matters they hear and question in the worship service: wives have their husbands and, by extension and in light of first-century culture, single women and girls have their fathers with whom to consult.

Accordingly, each version of contemporary complementarianism has its support. Without taking time to discuss them, each position also has its drawbacks. Tragically, constructive discussion of these positions is in short supply; what could be an important conversation has devolved largely into a strident and disrespectful debate. With so much ministry in which to engage, churches can ill afford to be racked by division and discord.

Diaconate

Added to this debate about men and women holding the office of elder/pastor is another dispute about men and women serving as deacons. As noted earlier, a key consideration is one verse in the midst of Paul's instructions about deacons: "*Their wives* [or *Women*, ESV mg.] likewise must be dignified, not slanderers, but sober-minded, faithful in all things" (1 Tim. 3:11). As Ryan Welsh and I note elsewhere, there are two understandings:

(1) This list of qualifications is for "their wives" (ESV, NIV 1984), that is, the wives of deacons. Along with their deacon-husbands, the wives of deacons must meet certain qualifications. (2) This list of qualifications is for "women"

(NASB, NIV 2011), that is, deacons who are women (deaconesses), like their male counterparts, must meet certain
(additional) qualifications.[15]

While there are good arguments on both sides, I think the
second interpretation is stronger, for the following reasons.[16]
In this part of his letter (1 Tim. 3), Paul sets forth lists of
qualifications for officers in the church. First, he focuses on
elders/presbyters (3:1–7): an overseer "must be" a certain kind
of leader. Second, Paul addresses deacons (3:8–10): a deacon
"must be" a certain kind of servant. Third, he turns to women
deacons (3:11): a deaconess "must be" a certain kind of servant.[17] This string of lists encourages us to view 1 Timothy
3:11 as addressing the office of deaconess rather than being
about wives of deacons.

Another reason for preferring this interpretation is that Paul
could have written "wives of deacons" or "their wives" if he had
intended to discuss that group. One might object that the ESV
cited above does have "their wives." Yes, it does, but the word
"their" is not in the Greek text; it is inserted by the ESV transla-
tors, who prefer (for legitimate reasons) the first interpretation.
A second objection: the ESV has "wives," and given the context,
it is clear that Paul is talking about the wives of deacons—"their
wives." Yes, it does, but the Greek word *gynaikas* may be translated as either "wives" or "women."[18] So it is just as plausible

15. Gregg Allison and Ryan Welsh, *Raising the Dust: "How-to" Equip Deacons to
Serve the Church* (Louisville: Sojourn Network, 2019), 12.
16. Arguments in support of the first interpretation include the shortness of instructions for deaconesses (we would expect more if Paul is addressing another church office)
and the interruptive nature of the verse if it addresses qualifications for women deacons
(we would not expect Paul to interrupt his discussion of male deacons to briefly mention
qualifications for deaconesses).
17. For a technical discussion of the Greek text and its use of "must be" and "likewise," see Allison, *Sojourners and Strangers*, 244–47; Allison and Welsh, *Raising the
Dust*, 14.
18. The ESV does include a marginal note recognizing that the Greek could be rendered simply "Wives" or "Women."

that Paul is addressing "women," that is, deaconesses, rather than "their wives," that is, the wives of deacons.

A third objection: If Paul had intended to switch from his discussion of deacons to a new discussion of women deacons, why didn't he simply write "deaconesses"? At the time of Paul's writing, the word "deaconess" did not exist in Greek. To signal his change from addressing deacons to another group of people, Paul simply uses the word *gynaikas*, translated as either "women" in reference to deaconesses or "wives" in reference to the spouses of deacons. If he had intended this latter group, Paul could have written "wives of deacons" or "their wives."

But Paul didn't communicate that way, which raises an interesting question: Why would Paul provide a list of qualifications for deacons' wives and not provide one for elders' wives? Assuming he sets forth requirements for wives as they accompany their deacon-husbands in their serving ministries, why wouldn't Paul do the same for wives as they accompany their elder-husbands in their leadership ministries? This absence of instructions about the wives of overseers is another reason for preferring the interpretation that Paul addresses deaconesses in 1 Timothy 3:11.

If this understanding is correct, then Scripture supports both men and women serving in the diaconate. Paul offers an outstanding example of the latter: "I commend to you our sister Phoebe, a servant of the church at Cenchreae, that you may welcome her in the Lord in a way worthy of the saints, and help her in whatever she may need from you, for she has been a patron of many and of myself as well" (Rom. 16:1–2). Additionally, the early church highly valued the ministry of deaconesses. They accompanied bishops on their pastoral visits to women members in their homes. Also, in place of bishops, they participated in the baptisms of women, whose clothes were removed before baptism to symbolize the removal of their old nature and their restoration to the innocence (nakedness) of Adam and Eve before the fall into sin.[19]

In summary, I understand Paul's instructions in 1 Timothy 3:11 to be a list of qualifications for women deacons. As leading servants, deaconesses do not engage in any elder-level responsibilities. They are not responsible for teaching biblical truth and sound doctrine. They do not lead the church overall. They do not have the duty of praying, especially for the sick (though they are certainly called to pray, as are all members of the church). And they do not shepherd the church. These are pastoral responsibilities, and they do not belong to women deacons. Accordingly, deaconesses may engage in ministry as leading servants, and they do so without violating Scripture (as argued in the above section on complementarianism).

In conclusion, I have explored *more ministries* by giving particular attention to the roles of men and women in ministry. My focus has been on whether both men and women may minister as elders/pastors and as deacons and deaconesses.

More Spiritual Gifts

All churches agree that the Holy Spirit continues to distribute spiritual gifts and that church members are to employ their gifts as empowered by the Spirit for the ministries of worship, nurture, and mission. Having rehearsed *mere gifts* of the Spirit, I turn now to *more gifts* of the Spirit.

Continuationism

Continuationism is the view that all spiritual gifts, including the "sign" or "miraculous" gifts, continue to be distributed by the

---

19. For further discussion of the roles of deaconesses in the early church, see Gregg R. Allison, *Historical Theology: An Introduction to Christian Doctrine* (Grand Rapids, MI: Zondervan, 2011), 594–95.

Holy Spirit and thus operate in the church today. These gifts are prophecy, speaking in tongues, interpretation of tongues, word of knowledge, word of wisdom, miracles, and healings.[20] Continuationism stands in contrast with cessationism (to be discussed shortly), which maintains that the above-listed gifts do not continue today because the Holy Spirit has ceased distributing them to the church.[21]

Arguments in support of continuationism include the following. First, the primary, though not only, purpose of spiritual gifts is to guide and empower the church's ongoing maturity and multiplication. The church still falls short on both counts and thus must continue to make progress in its holiness and mission. Therefore, the Spirit continues to give all his gifts, which in turn are to be exercised by the church.

Second, and enforcing this first reason, Scripture seems to indicate that all gifts will continue until the second coming of Christ. Specifically, Paul applauds the rich giftedness of the church of Corinth when he says to them, "You are not lacking in any gift, as you wait for the revealing of our Lord Jesus Christ, who will sustain you to the end, guiltless in the day of our Lord Jesus Christ" (1 Cor. 1:7–8). Similarly, Paul seems to locate the cessation of spiritual gifts—particularly those of prophecy, knowledge, and speaking in tongues—at Christ's return:

> Love never ends. As for prophecies, they will pass away; as for tongues, they will cease; as for knowledge, it will pass away. For we know in part and we prophesy in part, but when the perfect comes, the partial will pass away. When

---

20. For further discussion of spiritual gifts in a continuationist view, see Sam Storms, *Understanding Spiritual Gifts: A Comprehensive Guide* (Grand Rapids, MI: Zondervan Reflective, 2020).

21. For further discussion, see Gregg R. Allison and Andreas J. Köstenberger, *The Holy Spirit*, Theology for the People of God (Nashville: B&H Academic, 2020), 426–34.

> I was a child, I spoke like a child, I thought like a child,
> I reasoned like a child. When I became a man, I gave up
> childish ways. For now we see in a mirror dimly, but then
> face to face. Now I know in part; then I shall know fully,
> even as I have been fully known. (1 Cor. 13:8–12)

The apostle's reference to "the perfect" is Christ's second coming. At that point, partial knowledge will give way to full knowledge, limited prophecy will yield to full revelation, and dim reflection will be replaced by full sight. This "now . . . then" contrast is standard Pauline language indicating what awaits the church in the future: the fullness of the salvation that it experiences now in part. Until then, all the gifts continue to function for the upbuilding of the church.

Third, historical evidence points to the continuation of all the gifts in the church throughout its existence. Indeed, the "sign" gifts are strongly attested in the postapostolic church.[22]

Fourth, even during the apostolic age, the exercise of these "miraculous" gifts was not confined to the apostles. For example, Stephen, the first Christian martyr, performed wonders and signs (Acts 6:8). Philip, the evangelist of the Samaritans and the Ethiopian eunuch, engaged in exorcisms and healings (Acts 8:6–7). His four daughters were prophetesses (Acts 21:8–9). The Spirit worked miracles among the Galatian churches (Gal. 3:5).

Fifth, cessationism is incorrect when it limits the "sign" gifts to (primarily) the apostles and draws the implication that once the apostles died, those gifts associated with them ceased.

Sixth, continuationists ask, What would have signaled to the church that it should no longer obey the New Testament commands about prophecy and speaking in tongues?

---

22. For historical evidence of the continuation of spiritual gifts, see Stanley M. Burgess and Eduard M. van der Maas, eds., *The New International Dictionary of Pentecostal and Charismatic Movements*, rev. ed. (Grand Rapids, MI: Zondervan, 2002), 730–69.

> Pursue love, and earnestly desire the spiritual gifts, especially that you may prophesy. (1 Cor. 14:1)

> Earnestly desire to prophesy, and do not forbid speaking in tongues. (1 Cor. 14:39)

> Having gifts that differ according to the grace given to us, let us use them: if prophecy, in proportion to our faith. (Rom. 12:6)

> Do not quench the Spirit. Do not despise prophecies, but test everything; hold fast what is good. (1 Thess. 5:19–21)

No biblical directive instructs the church to no longer heed these apostolic instructions. And there is no such signal, proponents of this view argue, because prophecy and speaking in tongues (to name only two of the gifts) continue to operate in the church.[23]

Cessationism

Cessationism is the position that whereas certain spiritual gifts continue to be distributed by the Holy Spirit and thus exercised in the church today, the "sign" or "miraculous" gifts have terminated: the Holy Spirit has ceased to dispense them, and thus they no longer operate today.[24] Cessationism stands in contrast with continuationism. Importantly, cessationism does not deny that God continues to heal, perform miracles, and providentially direct his people today. On the contrary, he may sovereignly intervene in astounding ways whenever and with whomever he so wills. Cessationism, however, denies that God operates in such ways through believers who have received the spiritual gifts of healings, miracles, and prophecy.

---

23. Andrew Wilson, *Spirit and Sacrament: An Invitation to Eucharismatic Worship* (Grand Rapids, MI: Zondervan, 2019), 108.

24. For further discussion, see Thomas R. Schreiner, *Spiritual Gifts: What They Are and Why They Matter* (Nashville: B&H, 2018).

Arguments in support of cessationism include the following. First, the primary, though not only, purpose of spiritual gifts was to confirm the message and the messengers of the gospel at the founding of the church. How would the Jews, Samaritans, and Gentiles to whom the gospel was first announced acknowledge the genuineness of that message and the legitimacy of its heralds? Scripture answers that the good news of salvation "was declared at first by the Lord, and it was attested to us by those who heard [the apostles and others], while God also bore witness by signs and wonders and various miracles and by gifts of the Holy Spirit distributed according to his will" (Heb. 2:3–4). Signs, wonders, miracles, and certain spiritual gifts confirmed the validity of the message and its messengers. With the church's foundation laid (Eph. 2:20) and the authenticity of the gospel established, these extraordinary gifts are no longer needed for its ongoing development.

Second, Scripture does not specify a termination point for the distribution and exercise of the "sign" gifts. Many proponents of cessationism used to appeal to 1 Corinthians 13:8–12 (cited above) with the understanding that "the perfect" refers to the completion of the New Testament canon. "The perfect" arrived, and New Testament revelation was completed either at the end of the first century (when the last of the New Testament books was written) or toward the end of the fourth century (when the collection of the twenty-seven New Testament writings—the canon—was completed). At that point, the revelatory gifts of prophecy, speaking in tongues, word of knowledge, and so forth ceased to be needed. More recent proponents of this view agree with continuationists that "the perfect" refers to Christ's return, but they underscore that Paul's discussion of the partial nature of the gifts of prophecy, tongues, and knowledge does not specify an end point for these gifts. Accordingly, the determination of their cessation depends on other considerations.

Third, one such consideration is Paul's statement that "the signs of a true apostle were performed among you with utmost patience, with signs and wonders and mighty works" (2 Cor. 12:12). With this affirmation, the apostle seems to limit the reception and exercise of "sign" gifts to the apostles. This apostolic circle contained others such as Stephen and Philip, but even these men were apostolic-like or associated with the apostles. Thus, with these "miraculous" gifts being largely reserved for the apostolic band, once the last of the apostles died, the Holy Spirit ceased distributing these gifts to the church.

Fourth, this viewpoint is confirmed by church history. The historical evidence points to the cessation of these gifts at the end of the first century. The "sign" gifts are poorly attested in the postapostolic church.

Whatever a church's position may be, there are two errors to avoid. The first is an underemphasis on spiritual gifts:

> The church neglects instruction about and use of spiritual gifts, emphasizing instead theology, the Bible, and/or the officers of the church as those who are gifted and responsible for its growth. This practice robs church members of important biblical teaching and the exercise of their gift(s). And it handicaps churches from maturing and multiplying by means of all of the resources God grants to them.[25]

As for the second major error:

> The church overemphasizes spiritual gifts and/or they are expressed in ways contrary to biblical instruction. Prophecy

---

25. Gregg R. Allison, *50 Core Truths of the Christian Faith: A Guide to Understanding and Teaching Theology* (Grand Rapids, MI: Baker, 2018), 197; italics removed.

and speaking in tongues are often abused. Claims of healings and miracles, when unsubstantiated, lead to skepticism about sign gifts. Often, this position overlooks the teaching of Scripture regarding the purpose and use of spiritual gifts.[26]

To summarize, an important aspect of *more ministries* centers on the question whether the Holy Spirit continues to distribute certain spiritual gifts—prophecy, speaking in tongues, interpretation of tongues, word of knowledge, word of wisdom, miracles, and healings—to the church today. Continuationism answers in the affirmative, while cessationism answers in the negative.

To conclude this section, I've addressed the topic of the ministries of the church in terms of both *mere ministries*—what all churches believe about and practice in relation to worship, nurture, and mission—and *more ministries*. Churches diverge with regard to the roles of men and women in ministry and whether the so-called "sign" or "miraculous" spiritual gifts continue in the church today.

26. Allison, *50 Core Truths of the Christian Faith*, 197; italics removed.

8

The Future of the Church

The church acknowledges that its present, earthly pilgrimage is not all there is to its existence. A bright future lies ahead, beyond anything that the church can imagine or dream of. Indeed, for most of its two-thousand-year history, the church has longed for the return of Jesus Christ and the future events associated with that world-changing event.

Reminders of this future abound. Churches administer the Lord's Supper in keeping with Paul's forward-looking vision for this celebration: "For as often as you eat this bread and drink the cup, you proclaim the Lord's death until he comes" (1 Cor. 11:26). The divine purpose for God's people extends from eternity past (God has foreknown and predestined us) to our current experience (he has called and justified us) and into eternity future (God has glorified us, Rom. 8:29–30). This divine purpose is not hidden from the church. On the contrary, God has graciously made "known to us the mystery of his will, according to his purpose, which he set forth in Christ as a plan for the fullness of time, to unite all things in him, things in heaven and things on earth" (Eph. 1:9–10). Accordingly, Paul voices our firm hope: "I am sure of this, that he who began a good work in you will bring it to completion at the day of Jesus Christ" (Phil. 1:6).

All churches nourish this hope. But particular churches envision the future in different ways. This chapter addresses the future of the church in terms of both *mere future*—what all churches believe about and practice in relation to it— and *more future*. Specifically, hopes for the future are linked closely to views of the millennium. The four main positions are amillennialism, postmillennialism, and premillennialism in its two varieties—dispensational premillennialism and historic premillennialism. Each view has a different vision of the future of the church.

Mere Future

All churches look forward to events at the end of this age and the subsequent glorious future of the church. These events are the return of Christ, the tribulation and millennium (whether that is a present or a future reality), the bodily resurrection of the dead, the last judgment, the eternal blessing of the righteous and the eternal judgment of the wicked, and the eternal state of the new heaven and new earth. I present how these cosmic happenings relate to the future of the church.

Scripture often addresses the return of Jesus Christ as the church's central hope. Paul frames the work of Christ in terms of two "appearings":

> For the grace of God has *appeared*, bringing salvation for all people [the first coming, about two thousand years ago], training us to renounce ungodliness and worldly passions, and to live self-controlled, upright, and godly lives in the present age, waiting for our blessed hope, the *appearing* of the glory of our great God and Savior Jesus Christ [the

second coming, in the future], who gave himself for us to redeem us from all lawlessness and to purify for himself a people for his own possession who are zealous for good works. (Titus 2:11–14)

Indebted to Christ's saving work accomplished at his first coming, the church seeks to live in holiness and engages in good works during its earthly pilgrimage. Still, its purity is not within reach in this period but awaits Christ's second coming: "Beloved, we are God's children now, and what we will be has not yet appeared; but we know that when he appears we shall be like him, because we shall see him as he is. And everyone who thus hopes in him purifies himself as he is pure" (1 John 3:2–3). The church lives an already–not yet existence.

This glorious transformation from sinfulness into holiness, initiated with Christ's first coming, will be completed at his return: "Christ, having been offered once to bear the sins of many, will appear a second time, not to deal with sin but to save those who are eagerly waiting for him" (Heb. 9:28). On the one hand, this final judgment will bring eternal life and great blessing to the righteous in Christ. On the other hand, it will result in eternal death and great torment to the unrighteous outside Christ. As Jesus underscored, "These will go away into eternal punishment, but the righteous into eternal life" (Matt. 25:46). As the church from early on confessed in the Nicene-Constantinopolitan Creed about Christ's return, "He will come again in glory to judge the living and the dead, and his kingdom will have no end." The church has historically confessed its hope in this *mere future*, featuring the second coming of Christ and final justification at his great white throne judgment (2 Cor. 5:10; Rev. 20).

With apocalyptic imagery, the end of Revelation offers a captivating vision of the church's future:

> Then I saw a new heaven and a new earth, for the first heaven and the first earth had passed away, and the sea was no more. And I saw the holy city, new Jerusalem, coming down out of heaven from God, prepared as a bride adorned for her husband. And I heard a loud voice from the throne saying, "Behold, the dwelling place of God is with man. He will dwell with them, and they will be his people, and God himself will be with them as their God. He will wipe away every tear from their eyes, and death shall be no more, neither shall there be mourning, nor crying, nor pain anymore, for the former things have passed away." (Rev. 21:1–4)

The church is described as "a bride adorned for her husband." While during its present, earthly sojourn it is still tarnished and stained, the church in the end will be, and will remain forever, gloriously beautiful. Then and only then, it will experience in full the cleansing work that Christ accomplished on its behalf:

> Christ loved the church and gave himself up for her, that he might sanctify her, having cleansed her by the washing of water with the word, so that he might present the church to himself in splendor, without spot or wrinkle or any such thing, that she might be holy and without blemish. (Eph. 5:25–27)

Then and only then, the church will experience in full the perfecting work of the Holy Spirit. He is described as the first-fruits, the down payment, the deposit, the seal, and the guarantee of the church's redemption. These biblical expressions vividly picture his future-oriented work, which will include two monumental events: the resurrection of believers for their glorification (Rom. 8:11; Phil. 3:21) and the perfecting of the church's holiness and beauty. As for the resurrection from the dead, Paul explains,

> What is sown is perishable; what is raised is imperishable. It is sown in dishonor; it is raised in glory. It is sown in weakness; it is raised in power. It is sown a natural body; it is raised a spiritual body. If there is a natural body, there is also a spiritual body. (1 Cor. 15:42–44)

Reembodied believers will be imperishable, glorious, powerful, and completely dominated by the Spirit. As for the Spirit's perfection of the church, it will be washed completely and dressed in splendor, known as "the Bride, the wife of the Lamb" (Rev. 21:9). Until then, and in longing anticipation of that perfect transformation, "the Spirit and the Bride say, 'Come'" (Rev. 22:17).

Following Scripture, the church has historically confessed its hope in this *mere future*. In the words of the Nicene-Constantinopolitan Creed, "I look forward to the resurrection of the dead and the life of the world to come." Similar to this hope is the final affirmation in the Apostles' Creed of "the resurrection of the body and the life everlasting."

More Future

Within this broad framework of *mere future*, different churches look forward to different versions of end-time events and their relationship to the church's future. These different views correspond to the varieties of positions on the millennium as presented in Revelation 20. The four main positions are amillennialism, postmillennialism, and premillennialism in its two varieties—dispensational premillennialism and historic premillennialism. I treat each one in turn and show how each presents the future of the church.

Revelation 20:1–6

Much of the discussion of the church's millennial future centers on Revelation 20:1–6, especially the meaning of the expression "a/the thousand years" (italicized below):

> Then I saw an angel coming down from heaven, holding in his hand the key to the bottomless pit and a great chain. And he seized the dragon, that ancient serpent, who is the devil and Satan, and bound him for *a thousand years*, and threw him into the pit, and shut it and sealed it over him, so that he might not deceive the nations any longer, until *the thousand years* were ended. After that he must be released for a little while.
>
> Then I saw thrones, and seated on them were those to whom the authority to judge was committed. Also I saw the souls of those who had been beheaded for the testimony of Jesus and for the word of God, and those who had not worshiped the beast or its image and had not received its mark on their foreheads or their hands. They came to life and reigned with Christ for *a thousand years*. The rest of the dead did not come to life until *the thousand years* were ended. This is the first resurrection. Blessed and holy is the one who shares in the first resurrection! Over such the second death has no power, but they will be priests of God and of Christ, and they will reign with him for *a thousand years*.

The phrase "a thousand years" is rendered in Latin by the word *millennium* (*mille*, "one thousand"; *annum*, "year"). The nature of the millennium is debated. According to some churches, it is another name for this age in which the church exists. For other churches, *millennium* refers to a future period—many believe it will be a literal one thousand years—in relation to Christ's second coming. As I state elsewhere,

Historic premillennialism and dispensational premillennialism hold to Christ's return before (*pre-*) his thousand-year reign on the earth. Postmillennialism views this age as one of peace and prosperity, after (*post-*) which Christ will return. Amillennialism believes there is no (*a-*) future millennium but identifies it with the current church age.[1]

Amillennialism

Amillennialism is the position that there is no (*a-*) future one-thousand-year (*millennium*) reign; rather, the millennium is the present age in which the church exists. It extends from Christ's first coming to his second coming. Initially developed by Augustine in the fifth century, amillennialism succeeded the historic premillennial position (discussed below). Key to this view is its interpretation of Revelation 20:1–6. The binding of Satan was inaugurated during Christ's ministry. Christ is the one who entered the strong man's house, bound him, and plundered his goods (Matt. 12:29). The purpose of such binding was so that the church, unhindered by the (now-overcome) binding stratagems of Satan (2 Cor. 4:1–6), might engage in fulfilling the Great Commission throughout all the nations. Moreover, those who come to life and reign with Christ during the millennium are Christians who die and enter heaven to enjoy the presence of Christ. When the millennium, which is not a literal one thousand years, will conclude is not known. But Christ will bring it to an end at his second coming, which will be accompanied by the last judgment, the resurrection of both the righteous and the wicked, and the inauguration of the new heaven and earth.

---

1. Gregg R. Allison, *The Baker Compact Dictionary of Theological Terms* (Grand Rapids, MI: Baker, 2016), s.v. "millennium."

Thus, amillennialism identifies the millennium with this current church age and looks forward to the church's future in the new heaven and earth.

Postmillennialism

As I explain elsewhere, postmillennialism is

> the position that Christ's second coming will occur after (*post-*) an age of peace and prosperity (*millennium*) on the earth. Developed in the modern period, postmillennialism believes that the impact of the gospel will be powerful and very extensive, with much of the world's population becoming Christians. As a result, the world will be Christianized, or dominated by Christian principles. While not a literal one-thousand-year period, the millennium will be an age of righteousness, peace, and prosperity, after which Christ will return, execute the last judgment, and establish the new heaven and earth.[2]

Jesus's parables of the kingdom of heaven provide key support for postmillennialism. The kingdom of heaven, Jesus teaches, is like "a grain of mustard seed" and "leaven," portraying the slow yet steady growth of the church until its gospel and its influence on society eventually transform the entire world (Matt. 13:31–33).

Accordingly, postmillennialism identifies the millennium as a world-encompassing, transformative outgrowth of this current church age. Beyond this, postmillennialism looks forward to the church's future in the new heaven and earth.

Historic Premillennialism

Historic premillennialism, as I describe elsewhere, is

---

2. Allison, *Baker Compact Dictionary*, s.v. "postmillennialism."

the position that Christ's second coming will occur before (*pre-*) his one-thousand-year (*millennium*) reign on earth. As the consensus view of the early church, it is called *historic* premillennialism. Key to this position is its interpretation of Revelation 20:1–6: The great tribulation punishes the earth, then Christ returns to rule over it (while Satan is bound) for a thousand-year period. At its conclusion, Satan is loosed, then defeated in a futile effort to oppose Christ. The final events are the last judgment, the resurrection of the wicked, and the new heaven and earth.[3]

As in both versions of premillennialism, the historic variety holds that the church in some form will reign with Christ during the millennium period on earth. Still, there is a major difference between the two versions. Historic premillennialism holds that the church will suffer through the seven years of tribulation leading up to Christ's second coming. Dispensational premillennialism (discussed below) holds that the church will be raptured, or taken up to heaven, at the beginning of the seven years of tribulation. It will not suffer that horrific period of judgment.

Thus, historic premillennialism identifies the millennium as a future reign of Christ on the earth, with the church joining Christ in ruling. Additionally, this view looks forward to the church's future in the new heaven and earth.

Dispensational Premillennialism

As I outline elsewhere, dispensational premillennialism is

the position that Christ's second coming will occur before (*pre-*) his one-thousand-year (*millennium*) reign on earth. As a view developed by dispensationalism, it differs from historic premillennialism by its belief that prior to the

---

3. Allison, *Baker Compact Dictionary*, s.v. "historic premillennialism."

tribulation, Christ will remove the church from the earth (the rapture); thus, it is also called pretribulational premillennialism. Revelation 20:1–6 pictures Christ's rule over the earth (while Satan is bound) for a thousand-year period, which is followed by Christ's ultimate defeat of a released Satan, the last judgment, the resurrection of the wicked, and the new heaven and earth.[4]

As we've seen, this view, like historic premillennialism, holds that the church in some form will reign with Christ during the millennial period on earth.

Thus, dispensational premillennialism identifies the millennium as a future reign of Christ on the earth, with the church joining him in ruling. Before the inauguration of this millennial kingdom, the church also anticipates escape from the seven years of tribulation so that it will not suffer during that horrific period of judgment. Additionally, it looks forward to the church's future in the new heaven and earth.

In conclusion, I've addressed the topic of the future of the church in terms of both *mere future*—what all churches believe about and practice in relation to Christ's return and its associated events, such as the bodily resurrection, the last judgment, and the eternal state—and *more future*. Churches diverge on some aspects of this future in accordance with their different views of the millennium: amillennialism, postmillennialism, historic premillennialism, and dispensational premillennialism.

---

4. Allison, *Baker Compact Dictionary*, s.v. "dispensational premillennialism."

Conclusion

We know the church.

From the perspective of *mere ecclesiology*, we know the common ground shared by most churches throughout history. This is the essence, or core, of the church's identity, leadership, government, ordinances or sacraments, ministries, and future. We celebrate together these commonalities. When we visit churches other than our own, we sense deep bonds of solidarity. We perceive that we are with God's people, the body of Christ, and the temple of the Holy Spirit. We confess together that the church is one, holy, catholic, and apostolic. We feel at home as we worship with, nurture, and reach out with our brothers and sisters. We rejoice when someone is baptized with water in the name of the triune God. And we proclaim with bread and wine (or grape juice) the very basis for our gatherings: the gospel of Jesus Christ.

From the perspective of *more ecclesiology*, we know the particular expression of the church in which we are members. Our leaders may be bishops, elders, pastors, overseers, or some combination of these officers. They may be men only or both men and women. Our servant-leaders may be deacons only or both deacons and deaconesses. Our church's polity may be three-tiered or two-tiered, and our congregational members may have little authority or substantial authority in church matters. Infants may be baptized, infants and adults may be baptized, or only adults may be baptized. The quantity of water used may be sparse or significant. Our church may administer the Lord's Supper or the Eucharist or Communion or breaking of bread. This rite's relationship to the presence of Christ may be front and center of that celebration or not of importance. While our church believes strongly and practices its positions with conviction, it is also aware that these divergences can be stumbling blocks both to church members and to people outside the church.

Importantly, our church longs for the return of Christ, when all such divisions will be removed and will yield to unity. Then *the* church—ours along with all other churches—will be "the holy city, new Jerusalem, coming down out of heaven from God, prepared as a bride adorned for her husband," the Lord Jesus Christ (Rev. 21:2).

Until that glorious day, "the Spirit and the Bride say, 'Come'" (Rev. 22:17).

Further Reading

Allison, Gregg R. *Sojourners and Strangers: The Doctrine of the Church*. Foundations of Evangelical Theology. Wheaton, IL: Crossway, 2012. A deep book for more advanced readers.

Badcock, Gary D. *The House Where God Lives: Renewing the Doctrine of the Church for Today*. Grand Rapids, MI: Eerdmans, 2009. A deep analysis of the church from a progressive viewpoint.

Bray, Gerald. *The Church: A Theological and Historical Account*. Grand Rapids, MI: Baker Academic, 2016. An ecumenically sensitive approach to ecclesiology.

Ferguson, Everett. *The Church of Christ: A Biblical Ecclesiology for Today*. Grand Rapids, MI: Eerdmans, 1996. A New Testament theology of the church.

Hammett, John S. *Biblical Foundations for Baptist Churches: A Contemporary Ecclesiology*. 2nd ed. Grand Rapids, MI: Kregel, 2019. A helpful book from a historic Baptist perspective.

Horton, Michael S. *People and Place: A Covenant Ecclesiology*. Louisville: Westminster John Knox, 2008. A deep ecclesiology from a covenantal-Reformed position.

Keller, Timothy. *Center Church: Doing Balanced, Gospel-Centered Ministry in Your City*. Grand Rapids, MI: Zondervan, 2012. A helpful guide to church ministry in urban contexts.

Minich, Joseph, and Bradford Littlejohn, eds. *People of the Promise: A Mere Protestant Ecclesiology*. Lincoln, NE: Davenant Trust, 2017. A brief treatment of ecclesiology from a magisterial Protestant perspective.

General Index

Scripture Index

Short Studies in Systematic Theology

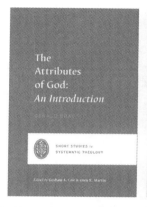

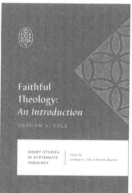

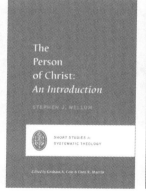

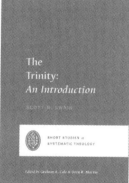

For more information, visit **crossway.org**.